The Creatrix® Method © Marilyn (Maz) Schirmer 2020

ISBN: 978-0-6483545-7-4 (paperback)

All rights reserved. No part of this publication may be reproduced, stored in a retrieval system, or transmitted in any form or by any means electronic, mechanical, photocopying, recording, or otherwise, without the prior written permission of the author.

Published in Australia by Marilyn (Maz) Schirmer and Amazing Media Productions.

DEDICATION

Dedicated to all the future little girls yet to be born on this planet, to break the curse of historic conditioning from being their destiny.

INTRODUCTION

Women suffer emotionally and mentally because we are female in nature and design.

We are often told we're crazy by the men we enter into relationships with, and even boys, just because we're not understood.

We start to believe it after a while and this strips away our innocent little girl confidence - if we were lucky enough to have a nurturing upbringing, which isn't as common as we'd like.

So we go to psychologists, counsellors and life coaches for help and for a while these things do help us and to some degree we can get relief, but some processes are just dredging up our insecurities and not healing anything ... So in circles we go.

When these things don't last, we take it personally and start to think we really must be crazy after all, everything doesn't work on us ... we think, 'it must be me'. We add this failing onto our already long list of things we think are not good enough about us.

Could it be that being female, our brain makes us not just see things differently, but feel things differently? Could our female brain internally process our thoughts in such a unique way that the entire personal development and psychology industries have missed??

What if I told you IT'S NOT YOU!

It's all a misunderstanding due to the traditional and even new age processes that are used today, all built on fundamental assumptions that a brain is a brain is a brain and therefore they must process everything the exact same way.

For centuries we've been teaching and using a one size approach that was initially designed by men. Could the brain that needs to run a cyclic uterus-central human need its own type of software that doesn't fry our circuits? What happens if you try to use android apps but you're an iphone?

Maz Schirmer hypothesised this and went back in history to the times when psychology was first discovered to see what they could have missed. In doing so she redesigned a psychological method to help women move forward, based on what she was able to uncover from her intense 13,000+ hours of research.

Initial testing proved her hypothesis right. She tried the process on males and it didn't work, yet for women it was causing an irreversible transformation.

Her process, unlike psychology, meant she needed little history, except to know how the client was still being affected NOW.

Then the client is taken on a journey with her eyes closed (to stay focused) and it's here she's guided through a storyline where she's so disconnected from any traumas, she's not even in the story. She goes on a voyage to solve problems for others of a similar nature to hers.

Strangely, when she opens her eyes, the wisdom gained by the stories' unique and specific characters, whom only she could have created, have transferred to be what she herself now knows without an ounce of doubt.

She's risen above her issues and now sees them in a mentally and emotionally balanced manner. She feels whole and balanced and healed. She immediately sees more choices in life. She feels hopeful about the future in relation to the issues she had and will almost always say she feels like she's had a weight lifted from her shoulders.

THIS IS CREATRIX®, UNIQUELY FOR WOMEN. You don't have to be messed up or broken, you can simply feel you are restricting yourself, holding yourself back or repeating patterns you no longer want to.

Creatrix® is the future of psychology. It's here NOW.

ABOUT THE AUTHOR

MARILYN (MAZ) SCHIRMER

In 2012 Marilyn (Maz) Schirmer opened the doors to the Institute of Women International™ and started training ordinary, every-day women, in her uniquely female-designed process of Creatrix® Transformology®.

Her innovative process is available to all of us, and this book is about witnessing real women, just like you, who wanted to regain their self-confidence, self-worth and self-belief and create a better life, but were not getting results through traditional therapy or personal development methods.

The long-lasting, irreversible results that Maz is able to achieve with Creatrix®, surpassed anything else seen in the Personal Development Industry and afforded Maz an invitation by a Hollywood Film Studio to feature in their award winning docu-drama, "IMPACT" (world premiere launched 22 January 2021).

A far cry from where she started.

Maz grew up in a small town in North Queensland, Australia, and spent the majority of her life believing she was worth less than the chewing gum under somebody's shoe. She suffered abuse and suppression that ran 4 generations deep ... so how does a single mother of 4, on the pension, go on to REVOLUTIONISE the personal development industry?

Maz uncovered the SECRET that had been eluding the personal development industry for more than 100 years, when it comes to transforming WOMEN.

Today, there are more than 250 women across 18 countries, who share her passion and have joined Maz on her mission to set 10 million hearts free.

This book shares just a few of their inspirational stories.

KARYN DE MOL, 54

Long-term de-facto relationship and childless.

WHAT WERE THE THREE BIGGEST BLOCKS YOU USED CREATRIX® FOR?

I'm not good enough.
Afraid of putting myself out there and that no one is going to like me.
Afraid to be me.

HOW LONG AGO DID YOU HAVE CREATRIX® ON THESE ISSUES?

April 2018.

WHAT ELSE HAD YOU TRIED PRIOR TO CREATRIX®?

Coaching, NLP, Time Line Therapy, hypnosis, kinesiology, energy work.

WHAT QUALIFICATIONS DID YOU HAVE WHEN YOU TRIED CREATRIX®?

Master Practitioner NLP, Time Line Therapy, hypnotherapist, kinesiologist, reiki master.

PROFESSIONALLY, WHAT PROMPTED YOU TO SEEK OUT AN ALTERNATIVE TO THE METHODS YOU WERE USING?

I had found my passion of wanting to help others, but I did not trust my abilities and certainly afraid to ask to get paid for my services. It did not matter that I had spent thousands of dollars to get qualified, I never felt I was experienced or good enough to be paid for my services.

PERSONALLY, WHY DID YOU DECIDE YOU COULDN'T CONTINUE AS YOU WERE?

From the outside looking in, it appeared I had the perfect life. I had a professional accounting job, owned my own home and a partner who loved me. I had the ability to go out partying whenever I wanted with no responsibilities, but it felt like a superficial life. I had a mental picture of how life should be, but it was fuzzy and having no purpose was going to turn me into a boring and bitter childless old lady.

WHO ELSE WOULD SUFFER IF THINGS STAYED THE SAME?

I was the main one suffering. Having no kids I felt like I had no purpose. I was dying inside as I wanted more from life, looking for that elusive purpose and passion. Going out and partying was losing its sparkle and thinking I had no passion made me bored with life and therefore affected my relationship with my partner and my friends.

IF YOU DIDN'T CHANGE, WHAT DID YOUR FUTURE LOOK LIKE?

I would have eventually just turned from a happy-go-lucky, fun-loving friend and partner to a bitter and bored woman with no purpose and so basically would have given up on life to the point of not caring about anything.

CRUNCH MOMENT – WHAT WAS THE DEFINING MOMENT THAT MADE YOU DECIDE TO HAVE CREATRIX®?

I found Creatrix® through a passing comment and as I tend to do, I turned to good old Google to find out more. I watched all the videos and information and was intrigued, and I decided there and then that I wanted what Creatrix® had to offer. I saw the physical and mental changes in the people on the before and after Creatrix® videos and I felt in my gut it was my missing piece. I wanted it for my future clients but more importantly I wanted it for myself. I was registered and signed up for the next course within a month of hearing the word Creatrix®.

WHAT IS DIFFERENT NOW?

I have purpose and passion, which has given me a new lease in life. I have embraced my uniqueness, and I love myself. I now have confidence in my abilities and care so deeply about helping women restore the peace in their hearts. I know who chooses and trusts to work with me will benefit from my skills and therefore help them get back to their real self, living and loving their lives deeply.

HOW HAS IT IMPACTED YOUR LOVED ONES?

Having confidence in myself gave me the ability to live my life fully and my cup of self-love was overflowing so I had an abundance of love that could spread to my partner. This made my relationship with my partner stronger and happier.

WHAT IS YOUR BIGGEST MESSAGE TO WOMEN WHO HAVE NOT EXPERIENCED A CREATRIX® TRANSFORMATION?

If you are a woman over 40, asking, "Why am I here? What is my purpose?" Creatrix® will help you find the answers you seek.

Have you ever found yourself lying in bed asking yourself what has happened to your life, sleeping the weekends away not even bothering to get out of your dressing gown, just binging on Netflix and eating chocolate. If you are finding yourself constantly daydreaming of a happier, more fulfilled and carefree life, then let Creatrix® lead you to find your courage, confidence and clarity to make your life what you actually want it to be.

You are not alone, and it is not too late to release the guilt, anxiety and constant fear that plagues your thoughts. You are good enough!!!

You deserve to live YOUR life fully and be happier than you ever thought possible.

CLAUDIA KOEHOORN, 50

Happily married, three daughters, two grandchildren and a third on the way.

WHAT WERE THE THREE BIGGEST BLOCKS YOU USED CREATRIX® FOR?

Not worthy to live.
Pleasing.
Excluded.

HOW LONG AGO DID YOU HAVE CREATRIX® ON THESE ISSUES?

October 2016.

WHAT ELSE HAD YOU TRIED PRIOR TO CREATRIX®?

I've had therapy. I studied psychology, during which I worked hard on clearing myself from all the emotional baggage I gained throughout my life.

WHAT QUALIFICATIONS DID YOU HAVE WHEN YOU TRIED CREATRIX®?

Counsellor and psychologist.

PROFESSIONALLY, WHAT PROMPTED YOU TO SEEK OUT AN ALTERNATIVE TO THE METHODS YOU WERE USING?

I was frustrated by the fact that I could easily let people acknowledge their patterns and convictions. I then gave them coping tools and it was up to the client to use them or not. What frustrated me the most was that if we worked on a problem, the client would "give it a place" that meant they would "put it in a drawer and stay away from it" but the emotion they attached to the problem remained and when triggered, would take over again. I just couldn't solve that with counselling or therapy.

PERSONALLY, WHY DID YOU DECIDE YOU COULDN'T CONTINUE AS YOU WERE?

Because I realised that feeling not worthy to live was affecting my whole life in all areas. It wasn't always clear to me or other people but when this feeling was triggered, I overreacted as if I were about to die. For example, when a friend would cancel an appointment for the third time, I would tell myself, "Of course I'm not worth her time or effort", and I would withdraw, which affected our friendship.

My husband and I have maybe one big fight a year, and when that happened, I was convinced he would leave me because I wasn't worth his love and attention, he would be better off with someone else. I would cry and lie in bed for at least four days, totally wrecked.

When my boss declined work I did, for example, a project proposal, I would instantly feel like I was really, really bad at my job and totally forget about all the compliments and credits he gave me, which would cause me to behave really insecurely. It would take weeks to build up my confidence again.

WHO ELSE WOULD SUFFER IF THINGS STAYED THE SAME?

My husband, my children (oh my gosh, the example I gave them), my friends, my boss, and my colleagues.

IF YOU DIDN'T CHANGE, WHAT DID YOUR FUTURE LOOK LIKE?

I would react hysterically when having a fight with my husband. I would do anything to please everyone around me and forget about myself. I was always scared to lose my job or practice, would not dare to be visible in my personal life and in business. I couldn't help my clients get over the problems I was having myself.

CRUNCH MOMENT – WHAT WAS THE DEFINING MOMENT THAT MADE YOU DECIDE TO HAVE CREATRIX®?

I was talking to my daughter and heard her talk like me and saw her do exactly the same thing I was doing, working late hours, scared to make mistakes, pleasing everyone, forgetting about taking care of herself, and I was horrified.

WHAT IS DIFFERENT NOW?

EVERYTHING.

I feel worthy and that's what I radiate. I'm authentic and visible. I dare to choose for myself. I listen to my gut and act accordingly.

I quit my job, started my practice, and I'm a successful businesswoman. I set healthy boundaries for myself and others.

HOW HAS IT IMPACTED YOUR LOVED ONES?

My marriage has improved. We are so much more connected because I'm not scared to tell and share how I feel or see things. I don't please anymore. I can choose to put someone before me, but it is a conscious choice.

My relationships are great. I said goodbye to all friendships that were not healthy for me.

WHAT IS YOUR BIGGEST MESSAGE TO WOMEN WHO HAVE NOT EXPERIENCED A CREATRIX® TRANSFORMATION?

Give it to yourself. It will change your life AND your loved ones' lives. Realise what example you are setting for your children – they don't listen to what you say, they do as you do. Break the negative cycle; be the one you really want to be. Free yourself and future generations.

DAWN CHEN, 44

I've been married to my husband for 16 years, together for 25, with no children.

WHAT WERE THE THREE BIGGEST BLOCKS YOU USED CREATRIX® FOR?

I suffered from anxiety due to work and business stress. I was also feeling frustrated at how stuck I was in life, my career and especially with my business, which was not showing much results.

HOW LONG AGO DID YOU HAVE CREATRIX® ON THESE ISSUES?

November 2017.

WHAT ELSE HAD YOU TRIED PRIOR TO CREATRIX®?

I have tried NLP, numerous personal development courses, hypnotherapy, various modalities of energy healing, and meditation.

WHAT QUALIFICATIONS DID YOU HAVE WHEN YOU TRIED CREATRIX®?

I have a degree in Business Administration and was a reiki practitioner and energy healing practitioner.

PERSONALLY, WHY DID YOU DECIDE YOU COULDN'T CONTINUE AS YOU WERE?

I was getting very stressed each time the anxiety came. It was affecting my sleep and my work professionalism, as I became reactive and angry with almost anything, even simple questions or innocent comments from others. For example, my husband would just suggest going for a walk on the weekend and I would react rather explosively that I had lots to do and I couldn't spare time for such luxurious activities like him.

WHO ELSE WOULD SUFFER IF THINGS STAYED THE SAME?

My husband had a reactive wife who was upsetting him, and my parents had to face a daughter who was short-tempered whenever they talked a little more than usual. I felt guilty and disgraceful that I was treating my loved ones in a way that they never deserved.

IF YOU DIDN'T CHANGE, WHAT DID YOUR FUTURE LOOK LIKE?

I would have sunk into depression, which would have caused my career and business to go to naught. I would have destroyed my marriage too due to hurting my husband terribly where he would not be able to function normally as we are each other's pillar of strength. My parents would have been really hurt too and that could have affected their health as they would also be very worried about my behaviour, mental state and future.

CRUNCH MOMENT – WHAT WAS THE DEFINING MOMENT THAT MADE YOU DECIDE TO HAVE CREATRIX®?

My anxiety was increasing in frequency, and no way was I going to deal with it by taking medication and seeing a psychiatrist, when I knew mentally I was still sound as I was highly aware of my ability to make correct choices and restrain my behaviour when situations warranted it.

WHAT IS DIFFERENT NOW?

I went on to do my job well as a human resource practitioner and left when it was on a high. As for my business in energy healing and helping women with Creatrix®, I went on to win multiple awards such as Asia's Best Brand Award, Singapore Iconic Influencer, Asia's Woman Leaders Award and Pioneering Woman Leadership Award by World Women Leadership Congress between 2018 and 2020. I do get anxiety at times, but it only lasts for a few hours and so is much more manageable, as it no longer comes with anger, stress and frustration.

HOW HAS IT IMPACTED YOUR LOVED ONES?

My marriage and my relationships with my parents and siblings have never been better, as I am so much calmer, at peace and courageous. I am a lot more fun to be with; my six-year-old niece and three-year-old nephew always want my company and for me to play with them.

WHAT IS YOUR BIGGEST MESSAGE TO WOMEN WHO HAVE NOT EXPERIENCED A CREATRIX® TRANSFORMATION?

Everyone deserves the peace, calm and knowingness that is already residing within us. When a woman is calm, at ease and at peace, she brings the same to the people she lives and works with, impacting the world ultimately, directly or indirectly. Why wait another day to live the real you confidently, joyfully when the solution is available right here, right now?

ERIN DAVIS, 43

Married to my high school sweetheart. We have three kids and a cavoodle named Cosmo, who we all adore

WHAT WERE THE THREE BIGGEST BLOCKS YOU USED CREATRIX® FOR?

Not good enough – I always felt that I was never good enough for anyone. I wasn't a good enough mum and wondered what they did wrong to deserve me.
Hurt – I felt like my daughter was deliberately trying to hurt me with her words and actions.
Fear of being rejected – I would never say what I really thought because I wanted everyone to like me. I always kept checking in to make sure I was doing things the right way.

HOW LONG AGO DID YOU HAVE CREATRIX® ON THESE ISSUES?

November 2018.

WHAT ELSE HAD YOU TRIED PRIOR TO CREATRIX®?

I had read a few books though I never had any time and reading took too long. I listened to podcasts driving to and from work from women who were making a difference.

I also attended some personal development seminars, which got me fired up and excited while I was there but then I couldn't put anything into practice.

WHAT QUALIFICATIONS DID YOU HAVE WHEN YOU TRIED CREATRIX®?

Nothing – I am an accountant and have been working in that field for 25 years. I had no idea that I wanted to do anything like this at all.

PERSONALLY, WHY DID YOU DECIDE YOU COULDN'T CONTINUE AS YOU WERE?

For years my emotions were out of control. I would cry all the time – particularly at work, which stopped me from progressing in my career. I couldn't have a conversation or say what I thought because I'd cry or just shut down. It was like I was on a roller coaster – no one (including myself) would know how I was going to show up each day. Every day was different and the highs and lows were very high and very low.

On a particular day I had tried to spend time with the kids and no one was listening and no one cared. I ended up in the kitchen on the floor in the corner sobbing. I had got to breaking point. I was angry so I just got up and left. I could hardly see while I was driving because I was sobbing that much.

I realised not long after that though that I didn't want to lose my daughter. I had to do something. I didn't like who I was. I didn't know how I was going to change – I just knew that I couldn't keep going the way I was.

WHO ELSE WOULD SUFFER IF THINGS STAYED THE SAME?

My kids were the ones who wore the full brunt of my erratic, emotional behaviour. While my work colleagues saw me crying every week they didn't see the angry, hurtful mum I was. I didn't even act like that when my husband was around. Thinking about it now, I was ashamed of my behaviour towards my kids. I pretended like I was in control, like I was strong and had everything all worked out. What people didn't see was an emotionally exhausted, hurt and broken woman. I wasn't fun. I was always rushing and I felt like I was doing everything by half and nothing was ever good enough.

IF YOU DIDN'T CHANGE, WHAT DID YOUR FUTURE LOOK LIKE?

I would have had one less member in our family, I would have lost my daughter. I just didn't have the energy to fight anymore, I was done with her.

I would still be stuck at work feeling totally out of control emotionally. I didn't want to spend the next 10 years feeling like I was still doing exactly the same thing I had been doing for the previous 10 years but that's what would have happened without Creatrix®.

I'd still be searching for that purpose though not really having any clue as to what I was searching for. I wasn't content and really happy though I didn't know what it was that I wanted.

CRUNCH MOMENT – WHAT WAS THE DEFINING MOMENT THAT MADE YOU DECIDE TO HAVE CREATRIX®?

When I broke down that day and left the house sobbing. I was supposed to be able to cope but I couldn't. I've never ever felt that out of control before like I did that night. I knew I couldn't keep going the way I had been.

WHAT IS DIFFERENT NOW?

I'm happy and I have fun. I'm not so serious anymore. I don't cry anymore. I don't stay angry anymore because I get over things quickly. I don't sulk and shut down. I don't swear at my kids.

My son says to me now when I say I'm going to do some work, 'Are you helping other mums be happy tonight, Mum?'

At work, I am now thriving in my role as a manager. I am able to have the difficult conversations when required and I am more confident. I am able to stay focused on what I need to do without worrying about everyone else.

I don't feel like I'm searching anymore. I listen to other women and feel their pain, hear the struggles they are hiding. I really believe I'm here to help them see that they don't need to feel this way. I feel like my life has purpose and that I am able to make a difference. I'm able to show others that I'm just an ordinary mum who did find her 'thing'. I found me.

HOW HAS IT IMPACTED YOUR LOVED ONES?

My relationship with my daughter has healed. To believe that she really does love me has been the greatest gift. If I didn't do anything else with Creatrix® other than to heal that relationship it was worth it and I'd do it again in a heartbeat.

I'm able to talk to my kids about focusing on what they can control, saying nice things to yourself and how your words impact both yourself and others. I have been able to slowly teach them about their emotions and feel that the language I'm using with them now enables them to feel safe and loved.

My relationship with my husband has improved, as I'm able to be more present and engaged.

WHAT IS YOUR BIGGEST MESSAGE TO WOMEN WHO HAVE NOT EXPERIENCED A CREATRIX® TRANSFORMATION?

It's hard to explain how different you'll feel. It's the little things day to day that have had the biggest impact on me. It's the way I talk to my kids, the way I look at the world around me. I feel a sense of calmness and peace, which I hadn't felt before. I now feel like I'm thriving and not just getting by. I've found my voice. I now know what it is I want and I'm not frightened to chase it. You are allowed to make yourself happy as well as your family.

By helping me, I know I've saved my relationship with my kids. I almost gave up because I didn't know what to do – I'm forever grateful I didn't.

HELEN O'NEILL, 59

Single, with two adult sons and a darling granbubba.

WHAT WERE THE THREE BIGGEST BLOCKS YOU USED CREATRIX® FOR?

I don't belong here, I can't get it wrong, I don't deserve love or success.

HOW LONG AGO DID YOU HAVE CREATRIX® ON THESE ISSUES?

November 2019, after hesitating and watching for seven years, as I was too scared it wouldn't work on me.

WHAT ELSE HAD YOU TRIED PRIOR TO CREATRIX®?

Reiki, kinesiology, NLP, counselling, psychology, EFT, hypnosis, Time Line Therapy, Chinese medicine, Landmark, dance therapy, meditation, mediumship, shamanism, spirituality, nutrition, coaching, mentoring and various academic qualifications.

WHAT QUALIFICATIONS DID YOU HAVE WHEN YOU TRIED CREATRIX®?

Reiki, kinesiology, NLP, counselling, psychology, EFT, hypnosis, Time Line Therapy, Chinese medicine, Landmark, dance therapy, meditation, shamanism, nutrition, coaching, mentoring and several business and leadership qualifications.

PROFESSIONALLY, WHAT PROMPTED YOU TO SEEK OUT AN ALTERNATIVE TO THE METHODS YOU WERE USING?

Nothing was sustainable, no matter how good I was at it, nor how diligently I applied myself to every modality. I didn't feel credible as a professional as I wanted real and lasting change for my clients. I knew nothing fully worked for me, so could never get ahead as I didn't feel congruent and authentic.

PERSONALLY, WHY DID YOU DECIDE YOU COULDN'T CONTINUE AS YOU WERE?

If it wasn't for the absolute love of my sons and grandbubba, I would have given up and let myself slip away from life, as I couldn't see a way of not getting stuck and stopped consistently no matter how hard I worked.

WHO ELSE WOULD SUFFER IF THINGS STAYED THE SAME?

My sons couldn't understand why I kept relentlessly trying new things, working myself into the ground, yet I was alone, unhappy, never having any money and not doing all the things I really wanted to do. It caused a distance between us, communication became withheld, strained and not open as I was closed and pretending, trying to make things right.

I also felt enormous guilt in not being of service and making a contribution to all the people and communities in which I sincerely believed I could make a positive difference.

IF YOU DIDN'T CHANGE, WHAT DID YOUR FUTURE LOOK LIKE?

Bleak, as I felt so fraudulent, disempowered and unhappy. I couldn't see any point in living if this was to be my life, so I was confused as I knew in my soul that I was always here to play a really big game, to make lasting and positive change, to have a powerful voice of love, kindness and justice out in the world.

I was disgusted with myself and hoped no one would find me out, because if they knew what my life really looked like, they would never want to work with me. Life was a continuous spiral into daily exhaustion from trying so hard, self-loathing, anxiety and massive upset.

CRUNCH MOMENT – WHAT WAS THE DEFINING MOMENT THAT MADE YOU DECIDE TO HAVE CREATRIX®?

My closest and dearest friend died suddenly. We had made a promise to one another that we would always follow and live our dreams and goals fully. We shared a deep friendship and love with a commitment that we would always care, encourage and look after each other. She only ever saw the very best in me.

She died not realising any of all that we dreamed. Honoured as the only friend who went with family to lay her to rest, I looked at her in that coffin and couldn't contend that such a beautiful, loved, intelligent woman had died with a life unfulfilled. My grief and shame that I hadn't been with her when she died was unbearable.

I promised her in that moment that I would honour us both and live my life full of vitality, fully free, and that I would thrive doing so. I would make a real difference in the world and have nothing stop me from that commitment.

WHAT IS DIFFERENT NOW?

I live a two-minute walk from the beach, surrounded by nature, which really nourishes me. I have a new, open, and nourishing relationship with my sons based on authenticity and love. I am in full creation mode with my business, taking consistent actions that has me achieve awesome goals each week. I am working with clients that I love and get to witness them live their lives with vigour, joy and satisfaction.

HOW HAS IT IMPACTED YOUR LOVED ONES?

My sons get to witness their mum as a woman who goes after what she wants, who is courageous and vulnerable, who loves unconditionally and has a bodacious, fun-loving passion for life and people. They get to experience a woman who is true to her word, takes responsibility and is honouring the unique gifts she was born with. They see that this is the most liberating and authentic way to live a valuable and meaningful life.

WHAT IS YOUR BIGGEST MESSAGE TO WOMEN WHO HAVE NOT EXPERIENCED A CREATRIX® TRANSFORMATION?

Every woman is born with a wisdom that is intrinsic to the essence of their soul, and this unique and precious gift is meant to shine brightly and be shared.

Trusting the wisdom that resides within and allowing yourself to be free to thrive is your birthright. If you are not 100% living life fully from this foundation, then you have an obligation to your soul that you will take the actions to set yourself free from whatever constraints have you stuck and stopped.

You are a catalyst, a role model for every woman you come into contact with, helping them experience what's possible if they were to also choose to set themselves free and live their extraordinary, destined life.

MARIA MCGRATH, 48

Living on my own, childless, not by choice. However, I do have six nephews and four nieces that I love with all my heart!

WHAT WERE THE THREE BIGGEST BLOCKS YOU USED CREATRIX® FOR?

I was totally consumed with sadness and loneliness, because I had not found the love of my life or had the children I yearned for. All I had ever wanted was to be a wife and a mum, it was so easy for everyone else, why not me?? Turning 40, I felt like I had been hit by a truck, I was a failure, and totally grief-stricken that I didn't have kids to give all of my love and to have that unconditional love back. The emotional pain was unbearable, and unexplainable!! Everyone else had everything I wanted, love, partner, kids, connection, family! How could they possibly understand what I was going through? I found myself drowning in the grief, loneliness and sadness and was quickly losing the strength to keep fighting to stay afloat!

HOW LONG AGO DID YOU HAVE CREATRIX® ON THESE ISSUES?

April 2012.

WHAT ELSE HAD YOU TRIED PRIOR TO CREATRIX®?

I had tried just about everything I could get my hands on, spending tens of thousands on anything that suggested any kind of change, breakthrough or transformation. NLP, psychologists, counselling, coaching, energy healing like reiki, Bowen therapy, and kinesiology. I did lots of personal development, reading hundreds of books, attending courses and even travelling to big events with international gurus, hoping and praying to find something that would snap me back to life, to the person I used to be.

PERSONALLY, WHY DID YOU DECIDE YOU COULDN'T CONTINUE AS YOU WERE?

From my mid-teens, I had struggled on and off with depression. There had been no specific event or trauma happen in my life. I was just overwhelmingly sad, and it felt like there was a piece of me missing. I was always feeling worthless and not enough. So I would push people away, believing that their love wasn't real because I couldn't feel it, leaving me alone and lonely. In my 30s, I really struggled with the fact I was not married and I did not have children. I felt like I was a failure, and not a real woman as I believed that I should have kids, a husband and be settled in family life. I couldn't continue as I was because the sadness and overwhelming loneliness had become an unbearable pain that was not just in my head and heart, but my whole body as well. And I had so much negative energy that I was becoming so angry and resentful, everyone around me was being pushed away, or ducking for cover, creating deeper loneliness and disconnection. I started praying every night to just die in my sleep, because the emotional pain was so intense and heavy. I found it hard to do more than just breathe and survive. I knew I had to try something new or I wouldn't survive this endless emotional pain!

WHO ELSE WOULD SUFFER IF THINGS STAYED THE SAME?

I had isolated myself from so many people over time that I really had no one around me, other than my immediate family. But they really didn't see me much either and I tried to put a mask on and pretend I was okay whenever I was around. My heart would break thinking that Mum and Dad felt sad and sorry for me being alone, not having the family that I wanted, and that they also wanted for me!

IF YOU DIDN'T CHANGE, WHAT DID YOUR FUTURE LOOK LIKE?

If I hadn't found Creatrix®, I wouldn't have had a future. I would have ended my life, ruining the lives of all my family in the process!

CRUNCH MOMENT – WHAT WAS THE DEFINING MOMENT THAT MADE YOU DECIDE TO HAVE CREATRIX®?

I got an email just after my 40th birthday, telling me about an amazing new tool, innovated by a woman, specifically for women! This was different, nothing else I had tried had mentioned a female difference, and I was desperate to live, so I had to give it a go! And wow, am I glad I did!

WHAT IS DIFFERENT NOW?

Everything is different now. I feel whole and content in my life, in my mind, heart and body. I have love inside of me, for me, and that enables me to give love to everyone around me, instead of isolating myself and pushing people away with negative energy. I give all my love freely to my nieces and nephews, never feeling sad or thinking that I missed out, I am truly happy to just BE with them and give them all of me. They get the best of me instead of the shell I had become before Creatrix®! I am now feeling happy, excited for my life and motivated to help other women feel whole so they can give their love freely without pain or self-pity.

HOW HAS IT IMPACTED YOUR LOVED ONES?

Someone close to me just lost a brother to suicide, and I witnessed the shock, hurt, grief and pain that it caused her and her parents. I am so glad my family did not go through that because of me! We are all stronger, happier and closer now.

My sister-in-law recently commented that my influence has helped her two daughters grow their emotional strength and resilience over their teenage years, growing more confident in themselves, and becoming amazing strong, loving and kind young women. My family now feel my love and support instead of the sadness, anger and envy that used to ooze out of me.

I love that I am now capable of being a confident support and mentor to the people I love the most. I now have an inner strength that was not there before, so I am spreading love, confidence and self-worth to everyone around me, all the women who take time to know and spend time with me.

WHAT IS YOUR BIGGEST MESSAGE TO WOMEN WHO HAVE NOT EXPERIENCED A CREATRIX® TRANSFORMATION?

I believe that every woman needs to know and feel life after Creatrix®! There is NO other way that you can truly KNOW yourself, releasing any and all of the inherited emotional baggage, easily and painlessly, and then get all your OWN inner wisdom that brings you back to who you were born to be!

When a woman has total self-love, self-worth, self-confidence and self-respect, she shines a light so bright that she can warm the hearts of everyone around her! Making the world a better place for the next generation, and the one after that!

NAOMI GALLIANO, 38

Married with one daughter and two sons

WHAT WERE THE THREE BIGGEST BLOCKS YOU USED CREATRIX® FOR?

I struggled with feeling angry all the time. The anger would just take over and I had no control, which made me feel like sh** about myself (guilty and ashamed) because I was so easily triggered into anger by the smallest things, and I constantly took this out on my kids and my husband. I had a deep fear of being my true self, because deep down I believed I was not lovable AT ALL. And I never felt good enough to pursue my dreams of helping others, and as a result I suppressed my dreams and desires, thinking to myself, "Who am I to help others!"

HOW LONG AGO DID YOU HAVE CREATRIX® ON THESE ISSUES?

February 2019.

WHAT ELSE HAD YOU TRIED PRIOR TO CREATRIX®?

Counselling, psychology, energy healing, reiki, self-help books, personal development and healing workshops, meditation, changes in diet and lifestyle.

PERSONALLY, WHY DID YOU DECIDE YOU COULDN'T CONTINUE AS YOU WERE?

Two and a half years ago, our family business sustained a huge financial loss that threatened all that we had worked for. I had forgone my own desires to conveniently work in the family business, so it dawned on me that if it could all be taken away so quickly, my life would be better spent chasing my own dreams. At this point I remember picking up a self-help book that reminded me that I was the creator of my reality. I realised I was living my whole life for everyone else and I had put aside everything that was important to me. I was working in the family business in a job I hated, and my life for the past 12 years had revolved around my husband and the kids. This prompted me to reconnect with my passion for finding a way to release emotional blocks and limiting beliefs that were keeping me stuck and creating the life I wanted to live ON PURPOSE!

WHO ELSE WOULD SUFFER IF THINGS STAYED THE SAME?

My whole family was suffering because I was angry, miserable, moody, grumpy, impatient, and stressed, and I was yelling all the time. My family always got the worst of me while the rest of the world got the nice me. I didn't have the confidence to pursue my dreams of helping others so all those people I was meant to help would stay in their suffering if I didn't change.

IF YOU DIDN'T CHANGE, WHAT DID YOUR FUTURE LOOK LIKE?

My future looked angry and miserable. I was a terrible role model for my kids. I didn't see my marriage lasting if I stayed the same because my relationship with my husband was disconnected due to my issues with my anger and being unable to be my true self with him and share my dreams of helping others heal from their emotional pain. I would end up filled with anger, bitterness, regret and resentment towards all of my loved ones because I would never end up doing what I deeply felt I was meant to do.

CRUNCH MOMENT – WHAT WAS THE DEFINING MOMENT THAT MADE YOU DECIDE TO HAVE CREATRIX®?

The crunch moment was when I realised that if I didn't find a way to release my anger, guilt and limiting beliefs that were keeping me stuck in the same old cycle, I would never live up to my true potential. I would never be the person I wanted to be and have the confidence to pursue my lifelong dream of helping others do the same. I had to change or my life wouldn't be worth living.

WHAT IS DIFFERENT NOW?

I took the leap and started my own business helping women heal from their emotional pain with Creatrix®. I feel completely free to be my true self. I can stand up confidently for what I believe in and speak my truth in any moment. I'm not angry all the time anymore. I still yell occasionally but it doesn't have the venom behind it that used to be there because all that pent-up anger and the issues around it have been addressed. I feel confident and happy with who I am. Finally I feel peace in my mind, love in my heart and calm in my body.

HOW HAS IT IMPACTED YOUR LOVED ONES?

My relationship with my husband and all of my kids has improved tremendously because now I can clearly articulate my thoughts without being so emotionally reactive. I have the patience to talk things out with all of them instead of getting emotional and yelling. Better yet, I can be a positive role model for my kids and help them work through their emotions, AND they get to see their mum following her dreams and being completely true to herself!

WHAT IS YOUR BIGGEST MESSAGE TO WOMEN WHO HAVE NOT EXPERIENCED A CREATRIX® TRANSFORMATION?

Any woman who is struggling with the pressures that come with being a mum owes herself the opportunity to explore how a Creatrix® breakthrough can help her to feel like her true self again! To be honest, I had no idea how weighed down I was because I had gotten so used to living with it all. If you're struggling, you don't need to struggle and live with your emotional baggage anymore! Do yourself a favour and book in with a Creatrix® Transformologist® so that you can find out how YOU too can feel peace in your mind, calm in your body and love in your heart!

BELINDA SNEESBY, 41

Married with two kids.

WHAT WERE THE THREE BIGGEST BLOCKS YOU USED CREATRIX® FOR?

I felt lost, I resisted change and was anxious about not knowing what the future held.

I felt like I didn't fit in and that I was always wearing a mask; I wasn't being me.

I felt overwhelmed about managing being a mum, family, working and time for me.

HOW LONG AGO DID YOU HAVE CREATRIX® ON THESE ISSUES?

September 2019.

WHAT ELSE HAD YOU TRIED PRIOR TO CREATRIX®?

NLP, business coaching, reiki, naturopath.

WHAT QUALIFICATIONS DID YOU HAVE WHEN YOU TRIED CREATRIX®?

Town planner.

PROFESSIONALLY, WHAT PROMPTED YOU TO SEEK OUT AN ALTERNATIVE TO THE METHODS YOU WERE USING?

Nothing worked.
I knew that I was lost. I knew that I needed to change the direction I was going in but was anxious about what could happen. I constantly changed my mind and felt overwhelmed by decision making. I wasn't confident enough in myself to trust in my gut. I needed an alternate approach, something that helped me to stop questioning everything and trust in myself again, to connect back into who I am and take control.

PERSONALLY, WHY DID YOU DECIDE YOU COULDN'T CONTINUE AS YOU WERE?

I was tired of constantly thinking, constantly rushing, not living in the present and feeling like there was always something missing. I wanted to find my something. I wanted to be happy with where I was right now. I didn't want to change who I was anymore to suit other people and feel guilty for just being me.

WHO ELSE WOULD SUFFER IF THINGS STAYED THE SAME?

My husband. I was constantly seeking reassurance and talking about what I/we 'could' do.

My children. I found myself being frustrated with the little things that didn't really matter and then feeling guilty afterwards.

Family. I would rush from one thing to the next, we all did. I felt overwhelmed and instead of being able to enjoy an outing, we ended up tired, cranky and not actually taking the time to be present and just have fun.

IF YOU DIDN'T CHANGE, WHAT DID YOUR FUTURE LOOK LIKE?

This is a hard question to reflect on. For me now, I feel like I fit, I am confident, I know where I want to be and for the first time in my life, I am not searching.

If I hadn't trusted in my gut, I would still be searching. I would be holding on to the little things, I would continue to feel guilty about standing up for myself and resisting change. I would be constantly searching for me.

CRUNCH MOMENT – WHAT WAS THE DEFINING MOMENT THAT MADE YOU DECIDE TO HAVE CREATRIX®?

After I spoke with one of the Institute of Women International head trainers, something inside of me just knew that this is what I had to do, this was my chance of connecting back to me, this was what I needed to find out who I was and move forward.

WHAT IS DIFFERENT NOW?

I know who I am and what I want. I am not frightened of what others think of me, and I trust in my gut. As a family we still have emotions; that's normal and we are able to resolve what is happening and move on without feeling overwhelmed and guilty. We laugh more, we rush less, and we are more present.

HOW HAS IT IMPACTED YOUR LOVED ONES?

I feel that by healing myself, I have started the healing process for my entire family. When I am strong and confident, so is my family. When I am not rushing and am calm, family life flows more easily. We are more relaxed and open with each other. We are supporting each other to chase our dreams, to believe in ourselves and each other.

WHAT IS YOUR BIGGEST MESSAGE TO WOMEN WHO HAVE NOT EXPERIENCED A CREATRIX® TRANSFORMATION?

If you know you're ready, don't wait. Trust yourself. Creatrix® is a game changer. You won't be disappointed.

HELEN PRICE, 45

I'm single and living alone with my two kids, aged 11 and 13. Plus the pooch!

WHAT WERE THE THREE BIGGEST BLOCKS YOU USED CREATRIX® FOR?

Before Creatrix®, I felt everyone else deserved to come before me. I was full of anxiety, heartbroken, and felt worthless – a burden and unwanted.

HOW LONG AGO DID YOU HAVE CREATRIX® ON THESE ISSUES?

May 2018.

WHAT ELSE HAD YOU TRIED PRIOR TO CREATRIX®?

I'd tried counselling, hypnotherapy, self-help books, webinars/online courses, spiritual guidance, crystals.

PERSONALLY, WHY DID YOU DECIDE YOU COULDN'T CONTINUE AS YOU WERE?

I knew I couldn't keep on going the way I was. I was a wreck and no good to anyone. Every time I got better, I'd go through the same cycle and end up crushed again. I felt completely lost and felt I was a useless parent. My son was also suffering from depression and mood swings and would constantly lash out. I'd lost my little boy. I needed to be stronger for him. Everything kept spiralling out of control and I'd just crumble.

I kept getting into poor relationships with narcissists who took advantage and drained my soul, leaving me full of anxiety and depression. I was full of sadness and fear. My self-worth was nowhere to be seen! I'd hit rock bottom.

WHO ELSE WOULD SUFFER IF THINGS STAYED THE SAME?

My parents were trying to support me and help me. They were always worried about me. Mom is not in the best of health and the stress was not good for her.

I wasn't able to be the supportive parent my children needed. I'd lose my temper with them over stupid stuff too. Snapping at them because my mind just couldn't cope. I felt like my mind was in overload.

IF YOU DIDN'T CHANGE, WHAT DID YOUR FUTURE LOOK LIKE?

I dread to think where I'd be now if I'd not found Creatrix®. I would've been stuck, feeling worthless. In my mind I would've been that burden on the world that no one needed or wanted in their life. I had gotten to the point where I didn't want to go on, so maybe I would've disappeared altogether.

I'm grateful that I never had the chance to find out.

CRUNCH MOMENT – WHAT WAS THE DEFINING MOMENT THAT MADE YOU DECIDE TO HAVE CREATRIX®?

I was desperately wanting more and wanted to be able to fill the aching hole inside of me. I was becoming increasingly dragged down by the fact that I was unable to feel any emotions, good or bad. I'd numbed myself to as much emotion as possible so I wouldn't feel pain, and in doing so, I'd stopped being able to feel happy too.

At the time I thought I'd lost the love of my life because I'd disappeared down a dark hole again. That ever-arising cycle of pain that seemed to follow me. The future I wanted and thought I had within my grasp had just disappeared again! I blamed everything on myself. I was speaking so vilely to myself in such a way I'd never dream of speaking to anyone else! Yet in reality, it was the narcissist partner that had just manipulated me into believing that. I'd been an easy target for him, as I'd already been beaten down in other relationships. Each time my self-worth was getting lower and lower.

I knew I needed to claw myself out of it, because facing the future as I was, was more scary than the change that was necessary to get myself out of it.

WHAT IS DIFFERENT NOW?

Now, I'm always in control of my emotions. Nothing really phases me anymore. I can stay calm in stressful situations and trust the decisions I make. I no longer feel like a burden. I know I make a difference. I no longer need others to like me to confirm my worthiness. I'm full of self-love, having found my inner happiness again – I'm truly HAPPY and no longer wearing the old fake smile to try to fool everyone! My heart is well and truly healed and I no longer feel the need to have a man by my side to provide me with the life I want or the validation that I matter. I know I deserve better and I'm in no rush to find anyone because I know I will never just settle ever again!

HOW HAS IT IMPACTED YOUR LOVED ONES?

Since I've healed myself, we are so much closer as a family unit. I'm making much better decisions as a parent. Both of my children are a lot stronger and more confident now. This is a ripple effect of watching me handle everything without anxiety and feeling confident to give them their wings to fly, instead of being the over-protective mom who always worried that the worst would happen if she let them go.

I'm also able to be there for my parents when they need me, rather than them needing to be there for me. As they get older, I know that I will be strong enough to be the daughter they need and can rely on.

We all have much stronger bonds than we did before and that's because stress, fear and anger are rare emotions for me to experience now, as the triggers are no longer there. So when someone else is stressed, upset or angry, I'm the one who is able to calm them down, rather than be triggered by them.

WHAT IS YOUR BIGGEST MESSAGE TO WOMEN WHO HAVE NOT EXPERIENCED A CREATRIX® TRANSFORMATION?

The pain of living with a broken heart means that you will never be truly LIVING your life. We are here to fill the world with love and happiness. How can we do that if we don't have that inside of us to share? With Creatrix®, you can release the pain from the past, and the fear for the future, to take life by the horns and ride it for all it's worth, the way that we were intended to live! We can stay true to ourselves and our passions, not bruised and hurt, forever fearful of experiencing more pain.

Why choose to stay stuck with that vicious inner critic when you can set yourself free?

The impact it will have on the rest of your life is priceless!! The ripple effect will start a tidal wave of positivity all around you!

You deserve to find your inner calm, to have complete trust in yourself and your decisions, to be living a life that is true to you. To be HAPPY, strong and free, full of self-love and fully respecting your own self-worth. To completely let go of the past so it doesn't rule your future.

Your family and loved ones deserve the best of you. A healed you will lead to a healed family whose bonds will be stronger than ever, and by healing yourself, you are stopping the cycles of pain and emotional torment from being passed down through the generations. It may not have started with you, but you can definitely choose to be the one to end it.

JULIE-ANN LANE, 58

Married with a blended family of six kids and seven grandchildren.

WHAT WERE THE THREE BIGGEST BLOCKS YOU USED CREATRIX® FOR?

I always felt that I was never good enough. I carried a deep shame with me. Grief was something that I carried as well, having lost my daughter 27 years before finding Creatrix®. Sadness was always with me. These issues were 10/10 for me.

HOW LONG AGO DID YOU HAVE CREATRIX® ON THESE ISSUES?

February 2019.

WHAT ELSE HAD YOU TRIED PRIOR TO CREATRIX®?

Self-help books, meditations, psychic healings, NLP.

PERSONALLY, WHY DID YOU DECIDE YOU COULDN'T CONTINUE AS YOU WERE?

I was 56 years old and very aware that I was not being who I truly was, like it was a watered-down version of myself that I was showing or offering to others, hiding behind fears and a sense that I was not good enough. I was not being my true authentic self.

WHO ELSE WOULD SUFFER IF THINGS STAYED THE SAME?

Everyone!

IF YOU DIDN'T CHANGE, WHAT DID YOUR FUTURE LOOK LIKE?

Beige, a dull, boring beige, lacking any colour! Uninteresting and uninspiring. Removing those blocks allowed the true me to shine through and it also allowed me the confidence to reach out for things I wanted or to say no to things that I did not want or wish to do, where previously, I would have agreed, just in case people didn't like me or I made too many waves by pushing back or just simply standing in my own space.

CRUNCH MOMENT – WHAT WAS THE DEFINING MOMENT THAT MADE YOU DECIDE TO HAVE CREATRIX®?

Something deep within me responded to Creatrix® when I was looking into it; it just rang true to me.

WHAT IS DIFFERENT NOW?

I have so much more confidence now, just to simply be unapologetically me. Without the nagging doubts that I'm not important or good enough to voice my opinion or to have people listen to me. I have moved beyond having the sadness of the death of my daughter surround me daily. It's not that I no longer have her with me, but it's with joy that I can remember her, without always that incalculable feeling of loss.

HOW HAS IT IMPACTED YOUR LOVED ONES?

I find my relationships are a lot easier. They just seem to flow better. I feel it's because everyone is getting the authentic me, I'm not hiding, and they don't have to interpret why they're getting a funny sense that I'm holding back or hiding a part of myself. So previously where there was a point where I sensed that people would back off me, you could see they were puzzled, they thought it was a problem with them, but in fact, it was me hiding, because I lacked confidence and was burdened by shame and felt that if people truly saw the real me, they would find it all too ugly.

WHAT IS YOUR BIGGEST MESSAGE TO WOMEN WHO HAVE NOT EXPERIENCED A CREATRIX® TRANSFORMATION?

We have the tool to break the negative emotions and cycles that have held us back and limited us, and that is exactly what we must do. As this not only benefits us, but EVERYONE that our lives touch, family, friends, peers, colleagues, acquaintances, everyone! Stand up and be who you truly and authentically are!

ANNETTE VUKOJE, 43

Married with two daughters aged four and eight years.

WHAT WERE THE THREE BIGGEST BLOCKS YOU USED CREATRIX® FOR?

As I grew up and as an adult, I always complained about people NOT SEEING ME for who I am. I never realised I had a fear of being seen. This fear was discovered through a Creatrix® breakthrough that had the BIGGEST impact on my life. Since clearing this fear, I can now have my photo taken, be on video, speak in public with no fear, lead a group in discussion and be part of social media advertisements about me and my business. I am seen, I am heard and understood, I can express who I am to others and they see ME.

Never feeling like I BELONGED to a group or with other people, then sabotaging any opportunity to be part of one. I always knew I did this to myself, but I never understood why. With a Creatrix® breakthrough, I was able to be free from the inner voice that would keep me as an outcast, and now I am eager to be part of anything when the opportunity presents itself.

Comparing myself to others. If someone else was doing what I did, I never felt I was good enough to do the same. I would have passionate moments and creativity, and I had the drive to create something to grow my business. But then, as I researched what others did and how, I would stop myself in my tracks as I would start to compare myself to them and their success. With Creatrix®, I cleared this issue and was released from the barriers created by comparing myself to others. I now see what others do and automatically flip it to think, "How can I do it better my way?"

HOW LONG AGO DID YOU HAVE CREATRIX® ON THESE ISSUES?

January 2020.

WHAT ELSE HAD YOU TRIED PRIOR TO CREATRIX®?

NLP, hypnotherapy, mBraining, public speaking classes.

WHAT QUALIFICATIONS DID YOU HAVE WHEN YOU TRIED CREATRIX®?

Master NLP, master hypnotherapist, mBraining, diploma in life coaching, small business management.

PROFESSIONALLY, WHAT PROMPTED YOU TO SEEK OUT AN ALTERNATIVE TO THE METHODS YOU WERE USING?

I felt I was missing something, a tool or modality that could help my clients more. I was not looking for help for myself; it was all about what else I could learn to be better skilled to offer the best service to my clients.

PERSONALLY, WHY DID YOU DECIDE YOU COULDN'T CONTINUE AS YOU WERE?

When I was doing the modules for Creatrix® I realised this was not about my clients anymore; it was about me. Even though I felt I had already cleared and dealt with my issues through my previous development training, I still had many issues that were holding me back in my personal life and in my business.

WHO ELSE WOULD SUFFER IF THINGS STAYED THE SAME?

What I could not see before I had Creatrix® was the impact I was having on my family, friends and people I worked with. I was affecting my daughters the most, by not allowing myself to play or becoming triggered by small issues that then affected how I interacted with them. My husband was always walking on eggshells because I could be triggered by something at any time and stay in a bad mood for hours. The trigger would be about something that didn't matter to us, so why did it change me so much? When we speak about what I used to be like, he always states, "I don't miss her at all!" We have not had an argument since I have had Creatrix®, and nothing escalates past a serious discussion.

IF YOU DIDN'T CHANGE, WHAT DID YOUR FUTURE LOOK LIKE?

I would have given up on my business and continued down a self-sabotaging path. My daughters would also be walking on eggshells around me as I would still be blind to how my moments of being affected by others would change who I was. I would lose the connection I had with my daughters and my husband completely and then blame myself for not being a good enough person, falling back into the drama and arguments that was once a normal part of my life.

CRUNCH MOMENT – WHAT WAS THE DEFINING MOMENT THAT MADE YOU DECIDE TO HAVE CREATRIX®?

When I first saw Creatrix® being advertised on Facebook, I was sceptical, thinking it was just another self-help course that would waste my money. Months passed and I slowly watched more videos from the Facebook advertisement, and I thought perhaps I would make an enquiry. The moment I realised I needed to study Creatrix® to become a Licensed Transformologist® was during a call with Bree Stedman about what Creatrix® does for women and how it works. It was in this phone call that I knew it was the missing thing I needed in my business. I had it on the front of my mind for months that with this training I could help so many women, and I needed to learn it ASAP! It took a very long time to come up with the money to enrol in the course, but I am so very glad I finally did it. I have no regrets and know that this was what I needed in my business and in my life!

WHAT IS DIFFERENT NOW?

The changes in myself are amazing! I have found the woman I once was, the woman who was spontaneous, passionate about life, carefree and fun to be around. I have discovered so many new things about myself that I never considered I could do before. I am the face of my business and have no barriers or self-doubt stopping me from implementing the ideas and strategies I create for my business to grow.

I am calm in the face of stressful situations. I am hardly triggered anymore, I have clarity in my choices and the ability to accept any criticism and see it as an opportunity to grow. I am a fun mum, and my eight-year-old daughter tells me often now that I'm the best mum in the world! She looks at me with pride and I believe she respects me out of admiration, not fear.

So many people have seen the changes in me and love how I have grown. I know they are a little sceptical about it still, but they will see over time that I can only get better with who I am and what I do.

HOW HAS IT IMPACTED YOUR LOVED ONES?

My husband is the happiest with my change. He has the woman he married back, the fun-loving me with no issues or drama. He can relax around me and not worry about when I'm going to be triggered by something. I can even see in him the love he has for me more clearly. My eight-year-old daughter wants to be around me more and asks me so many questions about the things I like, what was I like as a kid, if we can do things together, and she is more curious about mindfulness and development. My four-year-old daughter has matured more in the past few months as I have more time for her, and she is learning so much with me.

Things have changed with my in-laws, which seemed to be the biggest challenge for me in the past. My bond with my mother-in-law has strengthened, and she finally sees that what I do with my business is a real thing. We talk more freely and enjoy each other's company more. My father-in-law relates to me more and feels he can be himself around me. It's an amazing change to see people let down their walls because I have let down my own.

WHAT IS YOUR BIGGEST MESSAGE TO WOMEN WHO HAVE NOT EXPERIENCED A CREATRIX® TRANSFORMATION?

It may be hard to imagine your life any other way than the way it is now. And you may ask yourself, "How could Creatrix® help me be better than I already am?", or "How can Creatrix® be worth the high financial investment in myself when I have other family members to consider?" Or, a question I was asked recently, "Why would I want to remove my issues so easily, if working through them is the way people are meant to learn their lessons and grow?" I asked the same questions too when I heard about Creatrix®, and when I experienced it, I then understood why it is the most powerful transformation a woman can experience. It gives her ultimate freedom from her issues and results that last, allowing her to grow more within herself with clarity and direction for her true benefits to serve her best.

If you want more than anything to be happy again, enjoy life, to feel passionate, alive and free without the head chatter and issues blocking you from being yourself; if you want your children and partner to be happy and love you more for who you are and want to be around you; if you want to be the best version of you, the woman who can achieve what she puts her mind to, the woman who can face stressful situations head on with a clear mind, then ask yourself, "Why should I not transform with Creatrix®?" and if the answer gives you more benefit than what you really want, that's fine then because Creatrix® is not for you.

Just remember, the longer you wait to make the transition, the longer you will continue in the life you have right now. You NEED to do this for yourself and your family, so what's stopping you?

ARI POWELL, 40

At the time of my breakthrough, I was married with two children (I now have three).

WHAT WERE THE THREE BIGGEST BLOCKS YOU USED CREATRIX® FOR?

I was in a constant cycle of depression and anxiety. My biggest blocks were that I doubted myself and did not trust others. I was incredibly frustrated and felt constantly resentful of others and my circumstances.

HOW LONG AGO DID YOU HAVE CREATRIX® ON THESE ISSUES?

January 2014.

WHAT ELSE HAD YOU TRIED PRIOR TO CREATRIX®?

I had tried cognitive behaviour therapy, medication, a tonne of self-help books, and lots of expensive coaching.

WHAT QUALIFICATIONS DID YOU HAVE WHEN YOU TRIED CREATRIX®?

Teacher.

PROFESSIONALLY, WHAT PROMPTED YOU TO SEEK OUT AN ALTERNATIVE TO THE METHODS YOU WERE USING?

I was trying to grow my home business. I was working hard, and everything looked good on paper, but I could not achieve any of my goals. I had hired a coach to help me with strategy and systems to help me grow my business but made little progress. It was so incredibly frustrating. No amount of talking about what to do got me a result and I could feel I was holding myself back. For all of my outward appearance of confidence, I just couldn't get it together enough to achieve a level of success that felt like I was accomplishing something.

PERSONALLY, WHY DID YOU DECIDE YOU COULDN'T CONTINUE AS YOU WERE?

I had developed panic attacks and was struggling with workplace bullying. I was exhausted by constantly doubting myself, and I was spiralling into depression. My everyday life felt so heavy. I was experiencing high highs and low lows and the rollercoaster of emotions was grinding me down. I became suicidal and decided something HAD to give.

WHO ELSE WOULD SUFFER IF THINGS STAYED THE SAME?

My husband was supportive but bearing the brunt of my mood swings. My children had an angry, shouty mum, who would disappear to her bed for the weekend and was always too tired or too busy to play with them.

IF YOU DIDN'T CHANGE, WHAT DID YOUR FUTURE LOOK LIKE?

I was honestly scared that I might not survive, and I was certainly staring down the barrel of a tumultuous, deeply unhappy, and unsatisfying life. I felt trapped and angry and I did not want that.

CRUNCH MOMENT – WHAT WAS THE DEFINING MOMENT THAT MADE YOU DECIDE TO HAVE CREATRIX®?

I was driving home from work. I'd overheard some colleagues talking negatively about me earlier that day, I'd missed an important goal in my home-based business, I had been really struggling with every aspect of my life for a few weeks, and suddenly I caught myself strategically planning my death. I was shocked and decided I had to do something drastic. I had sceptically been following Creatrix® for about 18 months and figured I had nothing left to lose. I borrowed money from my parents to go and booked in.

WHAT IS DIFFERENT NOW?

I have not had a panic attack since my breakthrough, and depression and anxiety are a thing of the past. I finally started growing my business and achieved some of my biggest goals, and I eventually transitioned into a new business. We even managed to manifest a house and life feels amazing. The one thing I really noticed was the emotional strength I now have when dealing with what have been some extremely challenging life experiences.

HOW HAS IT IMPACTED YOUR LOVED ONES?

My relationship with my husband, which was already good, is even better. My kids are happy and healthy, and we have a loving and affectionate relationship.

WHAT IS YOUR BIGGEST MESSAGE TO WOMEN WHO HAVE NOT EXPERIENCED A CREATRIX® TRANSFORMATION?

You do not have to endure suffering to be a better person or achieve success in your life. You do not have to feel trapped and resentful. Your transformation does not have to be long and arduous. You can have the peace of mind and sense of fulfilment you desire within a month of starting your breakthrough!

BREE STEDMAN

I live with my young children and my husband.

WHAT WERE THE THREE BIGGEST BLOCKS YOU USED CREATRIX® FOR?

At the time I decided to become a Creatrix® Transformologist®, I was quite a successful leader of women significantly struggling with what most would call 'imposter syndrome'. Every time I would teach or train the women I worked with, I would beat myself up internally with a barrage of "You're not good enough, you don't even know what you're doing, you're like a little kid playing dress up in Mummy's clothes – why would anyone want to listen to you?" I would stand there, 'looking' the part with a big smile on my face, saying and doing all the right things, but internally beating myself up over all of the mistakes and errors I was perceiving that I'd made – and I'd compare how I performed to the other leaders in the room – pulling myself to pieces, because in my eyes I simply would never be as good as 'all of them'.

HOW LONG AGO DID YOU HAVE CREATRIX® ON THESE ISSUES?

I left imposter syndrome, feeling like a fake and a fraud, and not good enough behind in April 2013.

WHAT ELSE HAD YOU TRIED PRIOR TO CREATRIX®?

Access Bars, general personal development and leadership development training offered through the companies I worked for, cheap NLP courses and Law of Attraction processes I'd learned from reading countless self-help books.

WHAT QUALIFICATIONS DID YOU HAVE WHEN YOU TRIED CREATRIX®?

I came into Creatrix® with no formal qualifications – I'd become successful through experience and coaching, but I myself had never seen the VALUE IN MYSELF to invest in anything more than a $30 book – I was arrogant enough in my imposter syndrome to believe that anything I needed to learn, I would learn from on-the-job training, or I'd pick up for free from some other source.

I decided to train as a Creatrix® Transformologist® after having a personal breakthrough and recognising that everything I did know to help the women I was trying to help was so superficial that I was doing them an injustice to NOT invest in my training. And after my own experience and the dramatic improvement I had experienced with my own personal demons, I strongly felt that other women deserved the opportunity to feel as I did once I was free.... It was like I just couldn't imagine NOT being able to help other women at that degree.

PROFESSIONALLY, WHAT PROMPTED YOU TO SEEK OUT AN ALTERNATIVE TO THE METHODS YOU WERE USING?

I couldn't go on just 'giving advice' that I'd read from books, or regurgitating advice that I'd heard other leaders share.... For five years I had seen how limited this approach was – we could motivate our team in the short term, show them how to set goals, how to 'do', but we couldn't stop them from sabotaging themselves because of their head talk. I wanted to stop that cycle. I wanted to set my girls free from the BS they were telling themselves.

PERSONALLY, WHY DID YOU DECIDE YOU COULDN'T CONTINUE AS YOU WERE?

I couldn't keep 'leading' women, telling them to just 'fake confidence until you feel confidence' while I myself felt such little confidence. It felt far too hypocritical to continue to 'look' the part but not feel deserving, worthy or capable of it. I didn't want to spend my professional life living a lie.

WHO ELSE WOULD SUFFER IF THINGS STAYED THE SAME?

I believe that would have had a two-pronged effect – my family, in particular my husband, because every time I had an event coming up that I needed to present at, I would stress out – I'd lie in bed for hours thinking about what I needed to say and teach, so the next morning I'd be tired and exhausted, and therefore snappy – so the kids in turn were affected – they weren't getting the best of me because I was so hard on myself.

Professionally, I feel that if I'd stayed the same, I feel I would have burned out and quit – it would have been easier to put my head in the sand and find a job that didn't challenge me, than to fulfill what I have always believed was my calling – which was to be a leader. Either that, or I would have continued to 'force' myself to persist – although I can see that if that had happened I would have kept a wall between myself and my girls – and that's an inauthentic way to lead as well, isn't it!

IF YOU DIDN'T CHANGE, WHAT DID YOUR FUTURE LOOK LIKE?

I feel like my future would have looked very staged and therefore very unsatisfying and demoralising. After all, there's only so long someone can fake being ANYTHING other than what they are.

CRUNCH MOMENT – WHAT WAS THE DEFINING MOMENT THAT MADE YOU DECIDE TO HAVE CREATRIX®?

I was standing on stage being recognised as a top performer at our annual conference – my husband and my mum were sitting in the audience. Everyone was applauding and cheering, and I took my place standing alongside the other top leaders, looked around me and totally freaked out. I simply could not see how long I could keep up the façade – I truly felt that I was going to get caught out as a fraud, that at any point in time someone was going to come up, tap me on the shoulder and say, "Excuse me, Bree, we'll take all these accolades back, you don't deserve any of them because you're actually full of BS!"

I walked off the stage and burst into tears.... At the time I passed my tears off as 'overwhelmed with pride' but that night lying in bed with my husband, I shared my fears with him... that I was going to get caught out, that I'd fluked my success, that I couldn't make it last....

The next day when I was back training the girls at the conference, I couldn't shake the feeling of my inadequacies... I couldn't shake the lie I was trying to spin. That was when I knew that I couldn't tell THEM to 'just feel confident' when I couldn't find any of it within myself.

WHAT IS DIFFERENT NOW?

I've shed all the masks. When I train or teach at an event, I don't have a single doubt in my mind that I can't make an impact with my audience. I am so confident in my skin now – I've built my business to be an extension of who I am – perfectly aligned with what's important to me and who I believe myself to be.... Which in turn means I can give the very best of myself to the women I work with. There's NOTHING fake about who I am anymore. And this, in turn has helped me to show other women how to do it!

HOW HAS IT IMPACTED YOUR LOVED ONES?

Aside from the close, connected relationship I share with my husband, the greatest gift that has come from my decision is the role model I've become for my children – they were only young when I first started my Creatrix® journey, so in a way, they have grown up with me as I've emotionally grown up. They've become so emotionally resilient and they've also witnessed the impact that comes when Mummy steps into her true FULLEST self.

They are also growing up seeing how success can be built through focusing on others – I'm blessed that I've spent the last five-plus years travelling a lot to speak at various conferences and work with women around the world – people often say to my kids, "It must be hard with Mum going away like she does", and every time my daughter hears this, without skipping a beat she says, "No, because my mummy is helping OTHER mummies to be better mummies!"

WHAT IS YOUR BIGGEST MESSAGE TO WOMEN WHO HAVE NOT EXPERIENCED A CREATRIX® TRANSFORMATION?

A Creatrix® Transformation is something that rarely makes sense.... It's a decision that comes from the gut and the heart, that is driven by something MORE.... When I first had my personal breakthrough in 2012, it was because I wanted to be a better mummy – I wanted to be more for THEM. When I decided to train to be a Creatrix® Transformologist®, it was because I wanted to feel more confident in my skin as a leader AND because I wanted to give more for THEM – the women that I was wanting to help!

SO, if your gut and heart keep steering you back to Creatrix®, and you can see that by doing this for yourself, it's going to help you gain something MORE – more connection with your relationships, more success in your business, more impact in the legacy that you leave, then TRUST that and do it.

CASSIE MORRIS, 49

Married since 1992 with children, living on 10 acres.

WHAT WERE THE THREE BIGGEST BLOCKS YOU USED CREATRIX® FOR?

Shame, anxiety, unworthiness.

HOW LONG AGO DID YOU HAVE CREATRIX® ON THESE ISSUES?

December 2019.

WHAT ELSE HAD YOU TRIED PRIOR TO CREATRIX®?

Counselling; therapy; talking with mentors; self-help books; actually leading programs with children around protective behaviours; The Course in Miracles; human relationships education seminars through my teaching; inner child work.

WHAT QUALIFICATIONS DID YOU HAVE WHEN YOU TRIED CREATRIX®?

I am an educator at heart and on paper. My journey moved me into a leadership role in special education for fifteen years within a cluster of eight schools.

PROFESSIONALLY, WHAT PROMPTED YOU TO SEEK OUT AN ALTERNATIVE TO THE METHODS YOU WERE USING?

I have always seen myself entering into some type of healing role later in my career. I was looking into reiki, coaching as well as counselling just before I stumbled upon the Institute of Women International. What they offered in their course and the outcomes in being a Transformologist® were so appealing in my desire to help others and beneficial in my own healing journey.

PERSONALLY, WHY DID YOU DECIDE YOU COULDN'T CONTINUE AS YOU WERE?

Over the years I have been going down and thought I would not go up again. When I did, an awful uneasiness was beginning to rise within. Everything felt like a chore, without meaning. I was more resentful than ever and found it difficult to control these negative feelings that were swallowing me up. I knew I was on the edge and so began to search. I did not know what I was searching for but anything I tried, read and studied before gave me no satisfaction. Incompleteness was my mainstay. It felt like I was in a make-or-break situation in so many facets of my life.

WHO ELSE WOULD SUFFER IF THINGS STAYED THE SAME?

My marriage was the biggest weight on me. My partner seemed so unhappy and I felt the same. Blame was our constant conversation. I think that my children were under an enormous amount of pressure because of the uncertainty I was portraying.

IF YOU DIDN'T CHANGE, WHAT DID YOUR FUTURE LOOK LIKE?

If I had not been open to change, I would still be playing the blame game, hiding beneath my layers and frustrations. I was so sick of my own cyclic inner dialogue. Finally, I was willing to listen and take in something new. In fact, I welcomed it, which was not like me. I would still be on the merry-go-round if not for the Institute of Women International. I am sure my family would be broken, and anxiety would be my constant companion.

CRUNCH MOMENT – WHAT WAS THE DEFINING MOMENT THAT MADE YOU DECIDE TO HAVE CREATRIX®?

Everything I read and studied around the Creatrix® course made sense. As much as I tried to find any and every excuse I could to not partake, this time I could not procrastinate. I knew that I had to go this way, no matter the cost, financially or emotionally.

WHAT IS DIFFERENT NOW?

I am different now. I feel alive because I no longer have to run in robot mode. Everything makes sense. I am no longer in the Shame Arena. My safety has returned and so has my joy. The little girl who definitely protected me yet was my closest critic for the last 40 years is free to enjoy the sunshine and play outside. She is quiet and restful. I feel like I have come home, and I am complete. There is no missing piece within at all.

I have had to set boundaries for myself as well as others and I will need to continue to watch that. I deserve goodness. For so long, I acted and believed otherwise, and this catch-up process is part of my current journey.

The rewiring within is an adjustment mode I have to work through because of the fast-paced change that Creatrix® created. I have many other layers to peel off and I can, for the first time, accept that. The difference is, I have the inner strength and have found a way to tap into my own inner wisdom. I have my power back and that is worth more than any gold. It is the gold tried in the fire.

HOW HAS IT IMPACTED YOUR LOVED ONES?

Now that I am more centred, they can take a deep breath and relax more. Because I am accepting of my journey, I find that my interactions are more meaningful and calm. Because my Inner Critic is busy playing in the sunshine, I can hear myself, and others, for the first time. I am not so solution-focused because I believe the outcome will take care of itself. Anxiety is not my companion anymore. If folks want to dance when I dance, that is good and well. If they do not, that is fine too. I do not know the future, but I am happy with that.

WHAT IS YOUR BIGGEST MESSAGE TO WOMEN WHO HAVE NOT EXPERIENCED A CREATRIX® TRANSFORMATION?

Creatrix®, I believe, will change the world. The long-lasting transformations are happening at such a deep level within that future generations will reap the benefits. I am so grateful that I get to be part of this process knowing that my daughters will tap into their inner wisdom, power and confidence earlier than I did. I feel content and at rest. I am respectful in the same sense that a person has to be ready, completely sick of the old head chatter, desiring and wanting so much more. I want to shout it from the mountaintops. The power within feels amazing.

CATHY WHITE, 52

Married for 28 years and have three children.

WHAT WERE THE THREE BIGGEST BLOCKS YOU USED CREATRIX® FOR?

Feeling disconnected.
Anxiety.
Self-doubt.

HOW LONG AGO DID YOU HAVE CREATRIX® ON THESE ISSUES?

April 2018.

WHAT ELSE HAD YOU TRIED PRIOR TO CREATRIX®?

NLP, counselling, psychology, reiki, acupuncture, antidepressants.

WHAT QUALIFICATIONS DID YOU HAVE WHEN YOU TRIED CREATRIX®?

Life coaching, counselling, Reiki 1.

PROFESSIONALLY, WHAT PROMPTED YOU TO SEEK OUT AN ALTERNATIVE TO THE METHODS YOU WERE USING?

I didn't feel I had used the other methods I had learnt enough to feel confident to take on clients. I wanted to learn something that was easy to learn, quick to do and got long-lasting results.

PERSONALLY, WHY DID YOU DECIDE YOU COULDN'T CONTINUE AS YOU WERE?

I had always found myself in positions of leadership and even though I would do what was needed to be done, I would always have a lot of self-doubt about how I was managing everything and if I was doing a good enough job. I didn't like to upset anyone and this would all cause me anxiety. Although to the outside world it looked like I was confident with what I was doing, I didn't feel that way emotionally.

WHO ELSE WOULD SUFFER IF THINGS STAYED THE SAME?

My family was definitely suffering because when I was at home, I would over-analyse everything that was happening around me and go over and over it until I felt okay about a situation. I just wanted to feel confident in the decisions I would make and move on without ruminating on everything.

IF YOU DIDN'T CHANGE, WHAT DID YOUR FUTURE LOOK LIKE?

I would have continued to doubt myself and not have pursued what I really wanted to do, which was help women become the best version of themselves. I would have ended up looking for a job that wouldn't have satisfied my desire to show women that they can go after what they truly wanted. I really needed to feel it within myself first, so I had to get rid of the self-doubt and the feelings of not being good enough and not being worthy.

CRUNCH MOMENT – WHAT WAS THE DEFINING MOMENT THAT MADE YOU DECIDE TO HAVE CREATRIX®?

I couldn't stay dormant any longer. I needed to find something that ignited my passion to not only help others but to help myself. I needed to really feel like I was living life. I was talking to a friend who appeared to outwardly be happy and have everything she needed to enjoy her life, and I heard her saying she was seeing a professional for help. I realised that if we both felt this way there must be so many other women also feeling like this. This was the point when I knew I needed to find a modality that could help me and give me the tools to help others.

WHAT IS DIFFERENT NOW?

Now I feel really happy within myself and with the direction my life has taken. For the first time ever I feel content and I know this has had a positive effect on my family and friends. I feel like anything is possible and that I can help other women to find that within themselves too. I am on a journey of self-growth and discovery and when I come up against the next glass ceiling, I feel confident that I can smash through it. I now get to work with like-minded women and help other women find themselves again, so they can get on with living a happier and more fulfilled life.

HOW HAS IT IMPACTED YOUR LOVED ONES?

I have been able to help my daughter who suffered from anxiety and now she is confident and has accomplished some amazing things that she would have been too scared to try before she had Creatrix®. I know my relationship with my husband is so much stronger and I have been able to let go of a lot of issues and anger. I think it is important to show your children that the only constant is change and that we can continue to have self-growth. If something isn't working out, that we can find a way to change it rather than stay stuck. It has been easier to do this since having Creatrix®.

WHAT IS YOUR BIGGEST MESSAGE TO WOMEN WHO HAVE NOT EXPERIENCED A CREATRIX® TRANSFORMATION?

Women have an opportunity to change the cyclic family behaviours and beliefs when they have a Creatrix® breakthrough, freeing themselves from all the unwanted emotions, beliefs and behaviours that are no longer serving them. This is an opportunity to truly live life in a way that supports your highest good and it allows you to really enjoy everything you have and to help you make decisions that encourage a more fulfilled life. When you do that for yourself, you allow others to do it for themselves, which creates a happier and healthier life cycle.

DEBBIE EVANS, 59

Live alone with two grown-up children.

WHAT WERE THE THREE BIGGEST BLOCKS YOU USED CREATRIX® FOR?

After years of putting everyone else first, my cup finally overflowed because of workplace bullying. This left me diagnosed with severe anxiety, stress and depression. I lost all of my confidence and believed no one cared.

HOW LONG AGO DID YOU HAVE CREATRIX® ON THESE ISSUES?

March 2019.

WHAT ELSE HAD YOU TRIED PRIOR TO CREATRIX®?

I had tried a counsellor, life coach, psychiatrist, psychics, courses on self-development, gratitude and meditation.

WHAT QUALIFICATIONS DID YOU HAVE WHEN YOU TRIED CREATRIX®?

Life itself.

PERSONALLY, WHY DID YOU DECIDE YOU COULDN'T CONTINUE AS YOU WERE?

I was not getting results from my counsellor and life coach. I was sick of the tears, the stuttering and not being able to look anyone in the eye. I had lost all of my confidence, and I felt out of control emotionally.

I knew things had to change when someone close to me had their drink spiked and was sexually assaulted. I knew I needed to put on my oxygen mask first to be able to help them.

WHO ELSE WOULD SUFFER IF THINGS STAYED THE SAME?

My mother, children and friends were worried about me. My daughter thought she had to look after me. I had lost friends because I was no fun to be around, I did not go out, and I was wasting my life on lost opportunities. I kept my thoughts to myself because I did not want anyone to REALLY know what was going on in my head at the time. I felt like no one wanted to know me.

IF YOU DIDN'T CHANGE, WHAT DID YOUR FUTURE LOOK LIKE?

I had lost 20 years of my life feeling lost and alone. I really don't know where it would have ended at that point. I was tired of the fight and struggle and ready to give up. I could not see my way clear and had no idea of what happiness was.

CRUNCH MOMENT – WHAT WAS THE DEFINING MOMENT THAT MADE YOU DECIDE TO HAVE CREATRIX®?

I was at a conference focused on well-being. A presentation about females and getting rid of your BS resonated with me. The speaker mentioned a retreat she had coming up and I thought it would benefit my daughter; however, she could not go. I realised that I could only help my daughter if I helped myself first, so I was able to scrape together enough money to book my spot and it was the best decision I have ever made FOR ME.

WHAT IS DIFFERENT NOW?

The tears that ran in EVERY conversation abruptly stopped THAT weekend.

It was literally like turning a tap off. I now have difficult conversations in a calm manner. I don't stutter and I look people in the eye when I talk to them. I am able to talk to my children about things that I have always felt too scared to bring up. I am very aware of my calmness when hairy situations arise. I can consider my options and not feel like I am on a rollercoaster of bad situations. Even in the COVID-19 pandemic, I am VERY calm and I see it as such a wonderful opportunity for the world and the human race to heal and find peace and calm; to find a new way forward where we are not consumed by things that don't matter. Even having shut down our business because of COVID-19, I am not worried. I would have catastrophised everything two years ago, but not now.

HOW HAS IT IMPACTED YOUR LOVED ONES?

I feel like I am closer to my children. I feel they have benefited from the ripple effect of me changing. My daughter has commented a number of times and said that she is calmer and copes much better because of the change in me. She will have Creatrix® when she is ready for it. Our business went from the brink of bankruptcy 12 months ago to thriving and our books full.

WHAT IS YOUR BIGGEST MESSAGE TO WOMEN WHO HAVE NOT EXPERIENCED A CREATRIX® TRANSFORMATION?

I was at a point in my life where I had lost all hope of controlling my emotions, of stopping the fears and constant head chatter questioning everyone and everything around me.

I was so sick of it. I could see no future and felt worthless as a mother. I could see no place for me within my family. I felt that I did not matter to anyone, I never would, I was never heard, and I did not exist unless someone wanted something from me.

The after-effects of Creatrix® feel amazing.

The one thing that stands out for me is listening to Oprah Winfrey read her book *What I Know For Sure* on the way to my retreat and only hearing the terrible negative events of her life. When I turned it on to listen on the way home 48 hours later, I could only hear her positive message of what she has learnt from her life experiences. My brain had switched in the way it interpreted things in a truly positive way.

I remember not being able to get down to the beach quickly enough for a walk in the rain, of experiencing things in the last year that I can only explain as like bubbles popping and becoming aware of something amazing right before me, many long-forgotten memories. I want to do things I had packed away long ago, to enjoy friendships and develop my tribe. Being with family and friends now because I want to, not because I have to.

I am not willing to lose any more time wallowing in my fears.

Eighteen months ago, I was asked what made me happy. I had absolutely no idea. I thought that tangible things like a home would make me happy. I now know that is not the case. Happiness to me now is seeing something beautiful, feeling a wave of energy in my heart, smelling a favourite smell like rain on the dusty earth or fresh-cut grass or listening to music. It is simply Being in a space of contentment and Knowing you are there. It really is just so simple now.

Creatrix® has changed my life and I am so glad I stumbled across it. Don't let the fear of the unknown hold you back. Let the overwhelming heartache of happiness replace it.

DONNA BRENNAN, 48

Married with two beautiful boys, 19 and 15.

WHAT WERE THE THREE BIGGEST BLOCKS YOU USED CREATRIX® FOR?

Living with feeling NOT GOOD ENOUGH caused me to doubt everything I was doing, keeping me in jobs that I hated and feeling not good enough to learn anything new. OVERTHINKING used to rule my life personally and professionally, making it hard to make the right decisions. It was exhausting living in fight-or-flight mode. I would think of all the worst-case scenarios and play them over and over in my head. Any conversations I had with people would be on repeat.

FEAR OF SUCCESS: if I become successful, I will leave my family behind and not have any time for them. What happens if I can't handle success and I fail?

HOW LONG AGO DID YOU HAVE CREATRIX® ON THESE ISSUES?

September 2018.

WHAT ELSE HAD YOU TRIED PRIOR TO CREATRIX®?

Counselling, reiki, tapping, kinesiology, NET, 5 Second Rule, massage, acupuncture, Bowen therapy, exercise and diet.

PROFESSIONALLY, WHAT PROMPTED YOU TO SEEK OUT AN ALTERNATIVE TO THE METHODS YOU WERE USING?

Coaching women was made difficult due to the ongoing self-sabotage going on within them. I went looking for a vehicle that would get them faster long-term results. The only thing I could see stopping them was themselves and the negative head chatter.

PERSONALLY, WHY DID YOU DECIDE YOU COULDN'T CONTINUE AS YOU WERE?

I was exhausted lifting my legs out of bed. It was burning me out. I couldn't keep going without getting my own emotional mental state sorted first.

WHO ELSE WOULD SUFFER IF THINGS STAYED THE SAME?

My family would have suffered as my pain was getting worse. I was overthinking and I was out of control, which was causing me great angst as I was wanting to control everything. The people I was coaching said they could feel my own energy, which amplified their negative energy, causing them to sabotage as well.

IF YOU DIDN'T CHANGE, WHAT DID YOUR FUTURE LOOK LIKE?

My future looked bleak. I couldn't see a way out. Creatrix® helped with how I thought about things and changed my perspective. If I didn't change, I would have made myself very sick. My thought patterns would have gotten worse and mentally I wouldn't have been able to cope. My actions were not in alignment with my words. My dream of running my own business helping others would never have happened.

CRUNCH MOMENT – WHAT WAS THE DEFINING MOMENT THAT MADE YOU DECIDE TO HAVE CREATRIX®?

My brother-in-law passed away and my family was grieving. A few months later, I had a big argument with my husband and brought up 20 years' worth of hurt and anger; I was in blame mode. My body was in a world of hurt. This is when I realised there was more to all the pain I was suffering in my body. It was the realisation that I needed to change myself and only I could do it. No more suppressing my feelings, voice or anger.

WHAT IS DIFFERENT NOW?

Having a good work-life balance, I am able to spend more quality time with my family enjoying the little things, laughing, chatting and living in the moment. I feel happier than I have ever been in my life. I am more understanding and have let go of the overthinking and wanting to control everything, and I'm just living in the now. I'm running a successful business setting women free with Creatrix®, which I am loving. Fear of success, fear of failure and fear of not being good enough are all gone. I am passionate about helping others as I know what it's like to suffer mentally and physically, and be burnt out.

HOW HAS IT IMPACTED YOUR LOVED ONES?

My family has become more open and understanding than ever before. Changing myself has changed the energy in the household. I love being able to communicate better and see everything from a different perspective. No more getting angry at the smallest things. I am showing my boys that you can do anything you put your mind to at any age.

WHAT IS YOUR BIGGEST MESSAGE TO WOMEN WHO HAVE NOT EXPERIENCED A CREATRIX® TRANSFORMATION?

Finally, here is a vehicle that can easily and efficiently set women free fast. No more waiting to be the best that they can be. The benefits of Creatrix® makes us better role models, helping us change the epigenetic patterns and cycles into the future worldwide. It's our destiny to change the world around us and make it a beautiful place to live for all our children, grandchildren and the generations to come. Invest in ourselves so generations in the future will benefit by living a more fulfilled life. You will become confident and resilient with a new perspective on life. The world around you will look and feel different. If anyone is to break the PATTERNS, it's us. Rising to the mission of setting every woman free for all our children.

FEMKE VAN DEN HEUVEL, 52

I am recently divorced and live with my two 15- and 18-year-old daughters.

WHAT WERE THE THREE BIGGEST BLOCKS YOU USED CREATRIX® FOR?

My biggest issues were feeling like I was not good enough, I was not important and fear of failure.

HOW LONG AGO DID YOU HAVE CREATRIX® ON THESE ISSUES?

May 2017.

WHAT ELSE HAD YOU TRIED PRIOR TO CREATRIX®?

From 1995 up until 2017 I tried counselling with several psychologists for one to three years at a time. I also tried meditation, mindfulness, hypnosis and spiritual counselling.

PERSONALLY, WHY DID YOU DECIDE YOU COULDN'T CONTINUE AS YOU WERE?

I tried so many things for so long, and still I was struggling to feel better about myself. I was hiding from life, pleasing everybody around me, always criticising myself, always having a fear of failure. I was exhausted. I couldn't figure out how to get out of this. That made me feel hopeless. This wasn't a way to continue.

WHO ELSE WOULD SUFFER IF THINGS STAYED THE SAME?

I wished my daughters would grow up loving themselves and have a sense of value. I really tried to raise them this way, but I feared that I was a bad example and couldn't be convincing enough if I was showing them the opposite. You can tell your children anything, but the way they really learn at an unconscious level is following your example. So I knew I really had to change.

IF YOU DIDN'T CHANGE, WHAT DID YOUR FUTURE LOOK LIKE?

I would continue living a small life, hiding myself, not acknowledging my talents and staying safe rather than taking a chance and developing myself. I would be stuck and miserable. I wouldn't choose my own life, living it in alignment with who I really am, but letting others define me and walk all over me. If you don't choose, you are letting others choose for you. My daughters would probably grow up feeling the same way.

CRUNCH MOMENT – WHAT WAS THE DEFINING MOMENT THAT MADE YOU DECIDE TO HAVE CREATRIX®?

My best friend and I were watching her sister vlogging about her experience with Creatrix®. I know her, and in my eyes, she is a really down-to-earth person. She said, "I don't get it, this is so weird, my issues are really gone.

They are GONE. I can't feel it anymore!" I didn't know how yet, but it stuck with me, and I decided then and there this was what I needed. This was what I was searching for all that time.

After that, my friend experienced Creatrix® before me. I saw her testimonial where she said she remembered who she was meant to be. I craved to have that same feeling and I knew it was the right decision.

WHAT IS DIFFERENT NOW?

The biggest difference is my self-esteem. I feel really strong. I'm not considering myself less than others anymore. I stand up for myself. I don't criticise every thought and every move I make anymore. I shifted from trying to please others to pleasing myself. I make different choices, more in alignment with who I am. And from that, many things have changed. I decided who I wanted in my life and who I wanted to let go, even if that meant divorcing the man I was with for 27 years. It doesn't sound like something you want happening in your life, but for me it was the best choice. I finally could see this relationship wasn't doing me any justice, and I really felt I deserved more. Before I couldn't admit this to myself; I was afraid of the consequences and feared I couldn't cope on my own. Now I believe I can do whatever it takes and can do it even better on my own.

HOW HAS IT IMPACTED YOUR LOVED ONES?

The way I raise my daughters is different. I don't want to control them all the time, fearing something is going wrong and I am doing it wrong. I enjoy watching them become their own person and trusting all is well. This contributes to them feeling good about who they are. I can be a different example for them, and I already see they are so much stronger and more confident than I was at their age.

WHAT IS YOUR BIGGEST MESSAGE TO WOMEN WHO HAVE NOT EXPERIENCED A CREATRIX® TRANSFORMATION?

This is what you were looking for all your life. This is the only method that can change you to your core. And it is lasting. You even change future generations, so the impact is huge. You don't have to suffer anymore. There is a solution and it is so simple to do! It doesn't have to be hard, it doesn't have to take years and you CAN feel free!

HELEN PRINCE, 48

Married with three school-aged children.

WHAT WERE THE THREE BIGGEST BLOCKS YOU USED CREATRIX® FOR?

I was always angry, yelling at these poor little children then feeling like the worst mum in the world. And it wasn't enough to just be angry; I would find things to pick on that would keep me angry. It was like I didn't want to let it go because then I could blame everyone else for how I was feeling... it wasn't my fault; THEY were the ones that needed to sort themselves out and THEN I could stop being angry.

I was a stay-at-home mum for the first six to seven years and I really didn't want to go back to work doing nine to five. I really wanted to work from home and have a coaching business but was absolutely terrified of being seen. Whenever anyone asked what I did, I would quickly deflect the attention away from myself and back onto them. I knew in my heart that I was still so messed up, despite all the work I'd done on myself, so how on earth could I, in good conscience, expect another woman to pay me money to help her when I couldn't even help myself?

HOW LONG AGO DID YOU HAVE CREATRIX® ON THESE ISSUES?

September 2016.

WHAT ELSE HAD YOU TRIED PRIOR TO CREATRIX®?

LOA life coaching course
Abraham-Hicks
EFT
NLP
Hypnosis
Past life regression
Positive affirmations.

WHAT QUALIFICATIONS DID YOU HAVE WHEN YOU TRIED CREATRIX®?

Law of Attraction life coach.

PROFESSIONALLY, WHAT PROMPTED YOU TO SEEK OUT AN ALTERNATIVE TO THE METHODS YOU WERE USING?

Nothing stuck. I was okay when doing the processes on myself but as soon as I stopped, it all came back. I didn't have time to constantly be working on myself; I had three small children and I was working part-time. It was incredibly frustrating. I knew there had to be an easier way. It felt wrong asking people for money to fix them when I knew I couldn't do it for myself and that it would all come back anyway. If I wasn't prepared to put in the time, why should they?

PERSONALLY, WHY DID YOU DECIDE YOU COULDN'T CONTINUE AS YOU WERE?

I was always yelling, always angry, and I could see how it was affecting my children and my marriage. My pattern was to run away when it got too hard, but you can't just do that when kids are involved.

WHO ELSE WOULD SUFFER IF THINGS STAYED THE SAME?

I could see how my mood and attitude were impacting the kids. They would act up more when I was in a mood and that just made it worse. My husband retreated; he had to walk around on eggshells because who knew when cray-cray would come out and start yelling.

IF YOU DIDN'T CHANGE, WHAT DID YOUR FUTURE LOOK LIKE?

If I kept going down that path, I would have ended up with divorce number two and ruined not only my life but the lives of four other people. I would be this angry, bitter, resentful woman... definitely not the environment I imagined when we decided to have a family.

CRUNCH MOMENT – WHAT WAS THE DEFINING MOMENT THAT MADE YOU DECIDE TO HAVE CREATRIX®?

I woke up one day and realised that I hated who I'd become and what I was doing to our kids.

WHAT IS DIFFERENT NOW?

The house is a much happier place; yes, there are still arguments sometimes; we're all still human! Hubby has gone back to being his old self where we joke and have fun; it's like it used to be when we first met. I feel happier. I'm doing what I love and what makes me feel fulfilled and that rubs off onto everyone around me.

HOW HAS IT IMPACTED YOUR LOVED ONES?

We can talk about things without Mum yelling and them getting defensive. It's a more open and accepting environment.

WHAT IS YOUR BIGGEST MESSAGE TO WOMEN WHO HAVE NOT EXPERIENCED A CREATRIX® TRANSFORMATION?

It all starts with you. Women have more of an influence than we might realise. If we want the world to be a better place for our kids and grandkids, then we need to start with ourselves and be the example, be the role model. That was really important for me; I wanted to SHOW my kids how to be, not just tell them. At the end of the day, talk is cheap. Actions really do speak louder than words.

IRNA EVERS, 61

In a committed relationship; has two adult daughters.

WHAT WERE THE THREE BIGGEST BLOCKS YOU USED CREATRIX® FOR?

Fear of abandonment.
I do not matter.
I can't be there.

HOW LONG AGO DID YOU HAVE CREATRIX® ON THESE ISSUES?

June 2019.

WHAT ELSE HAD YOU TRIED PRIOR TO CREATRIX®?

Cognitive therapy, coaching, emotional body work, hypnotherapy, healing, education, Family Constellations.

WHAT QUALIFICATIONS DID YOU HAVE WHEN YOU TRIED CREATRIX®?

Communication advisor and events organiser.

PROFESSIONALLY, WHAT PROMPTED YOU TO SEEK OUT AN ALTERNATIVE TO THE METHODS YOU WERE USING?

I wanted to help women in the process that I had and couldn't find the right tool until I found Creatrix®.

PERSONALLY, WHY DID YOU DECIDE YOU COULDN'T CONTINUE AS YOU WERE?

Because I was burned out for the second time in my life and about to lose myself completely.

WHO ELSE WOULD SUFFER IF THINGS STAYED THE SAME?

The man who loves me, my children, my family, and my friends.

IF YOU DIDN'T CHANGE, WHAT DID YOUR FUTURE LOOK LIKE?

Very alone, unhappy, afraid, holding myself back and not living my life the way I wanted it.

CRUNCH MOMENT – WHAT WAS THE DEFINING MOMENT THAT MADE YOU DECIDE TO HAVE CREATRIX®?

I knew exactly what I wanted to do to help myself. That was doing the course of with the Institute of Women International. I had done my research, I looked up everything about it, I knew that this was what I needed but yet I didn't take the step, the step for ME. And I had a "kick in the ass" by my love. He said, "You are doing it again, aren't you? Not choosing what's good for you now!" That was the moment I knew: I'm going to do it now!

WHAT IS DIFFERENT NOW?

Life is good. I feel free, happy and light, and full of energy. I'm making new choices. I have a new way of life: my own practice, YourYou now, helping other women free themselves.

HOW HAS IT IMPACTED YOUR LOVED ONES?

My love tells me he sees me happier every day and he's happy that I'm taking care of myself now by making choices that are good for me. Our relationship always was very open and safe, like soulmates. And now it is so much more deep, intense, full and flowing.

Contact with my children wasn't good after I left my ex-husband seven years ago. I can accept it now without a lot of pain. I know I'm their mother and they have to learn their own lessons. And that's okay.

WHAT IS YOUR BIGGEST MESSAGE TO WOMEN WHO HAVE NOT EXPERIENCED A CREATRIX® TRANSFORMATION?

If you take care of everyone and everything, and forget yourself, you'll lose yourself. I know it's in your system, the thing that's holding you back in everything you like to do. With Creatrix®, you'll get rid of it. This makes you close with yourself (without being selfish), happy with yourself and strong in making your own choices and decisions that are good for YOU. It makes you a better woman, wife, mother, friend and colleague. It makes you the best version of yourself!

JILL MATHEWS, 57

Single, divorced. I live alone now, after devoting 20 years of my life as a single mum to two sons.

WHAT WERE THE THREE BIGGEST BLOCKS YOU USED CREATRIX® FOR?

1. Worthlessness. I was raised in England in the 60s when little girls were meant to be seen and not heard. I believed that women were second-class citizens and not worthy of having a career or an independent life. I felt that I was never good enough for anyone or anything. I was never satisfied with life, and unable to celebrate my wins. I found my first boyfriend at 18 and for the next seven years I suffered feelings of worthlessness. I was never good enough or pretty enough for him and ended up with an eating disorder which controlled my life for 14 years.

2. Sadness. I actually had what everyone else would perceive as a privileged life. I was brought up in a middle-class family in a magnificent part of England, with private school and university education, pets, horses and overseas vacations. However, I had this deep, deep sadness and feeling of total unfulfillment. I just couldn't laugh, couldn't see the bright side of anything, and I had this deep yearning to feel happiness. I couldn't understand

why, despite a good upbringing, I was so DESPERATELY sad all the time. I ran away to Australia in my 20s to try and find happiness, but the sadness followed.

3. Fear. When I became a single mother, the fear of life itself set in. Although I was well educated, had a home and a business, and was always able to earn an income and support us, life was terrifying.

4. Overwhelmed. I always believed that MONEY EQUALS FREEDOM, so I worked tirelessly, to the expense of all else, to keep working, running a business and having side businesses to keep money coming in. I was a single mum and felt completely overwhelmed with the constant juggle of family, home, income and business, as well as the pressure of having extended family overseas and the need to keep my sons in touch with them.

HOW LONG AGO DID YOU HAVE CREATRIX® ON THESE ISSUES?

August 2017.

WHAT ELSE HAD YOU TRIED PRIOR TO CREATRIX®?

I tried psychoanalysis, hypnotherapy, counselling, Enneagram training, kinesiology, mindfulness training, self-development books and courses, psychotherapy and kinesiology. Nothing seemed to stick.

WHAT QUALIFICATIONS DID YOU HAVE WHEN YOU TRIED CREATRIX®?

None. I was a teacher and small business owner, but never worked in the emotional healing business.

PERSONALLY, WHY DID YOU DECIDE YOU COULDN'T CONTINUE AS YOU WERE?

I just couldn't stop crying. I cried at everything. I was always scared, frustrated, angry at my kids and family and so, so sad.

I wore this mask all the time; on the outside I was this happy, smiling, helpful woman who seemed to inspire others. But on the inside, I was dying from unhappiness. I had no real reason to be so sad, but it was a controlling emotion that I couldn't clear.

Now that I know a bit more about epigenetics, I realise that this deep, unexplainable sadness was probably inherited. I just kept saying to myself, "What's wrong with me?" When I researched Creatrix®, I heard other women asking the same question about themselves. It took me only minutes to decide that I had to try Creatrix®, both to help myself and help other sad women.

WHO ELSE WOULD SUFFER IF THINGS STAYED THE SAME?

My two sons were suffering because of me. I was always shouting at them, even though it was me that I was angry with. They had already missed out on a lot of family interaction because of my issues, so I wanted to get control of my emotions so that I did not damage them any further.

IF YOU DIDN'T CHANGE, WHAT DID YOUR FUTURE LOOK LIKE?

If I didn't change, my sons would suffer more. I would have just spent the rest of my life in misery and self-pity. My business was suffering, and people were starting to complain because I was snappy and impatient with clients. I was spending insane amounts of money on self-help courses, books and investments in my financial future. I was trying all the time to fix what was on the outside, in my external environment and things that I believed were in my control. However, what I needed was to fix what was broken and unbalanced on the inside.

CRUNCH MOMENT – WHAT WAS THE DEFINING MOMENT THAT MADE YOU DECIDE TO HAVE CREATRIX®?

I had seen Maz mention this strange word "Creatrix®" on Facebook. One day I got curious and researched it. As soon as I saw a couple of videos online, I was convinced. I contacted Maz immediately and was all signed up by the same evening.

WHAT IS DIFFERENT NOW?

I'm just so calm and in control now. Yes, sure, I'm still an emotional female and feel things very deeply, but I don't hold on to it anymore. I feel the pain, lean into it, accept it and then move on. I was never able to do that pre-Creatrix®. All my friends, family and my sons noticed that I wasn't stressed and yelling any more. My business started to grow and grow. Now I flip to-and-fro between England and Australia, sorting my mother's affairs. I'm running two businesses and am content with the level that I've taken each business. The desperate desire to keep getting better and better and the awful feeling of never being satisfied has gone. I'm much more appreciative of the small things in life. My relationship with my two sons is amazing.

HOW HAS IT IMPACTED YOUR LOVED ONES?

I'm just able to get on with life now. I look forward to seeing my sons and we always have a relaxed time together. I don't nag them anymore and just accept their choices in life, even if I don't particularly like them. There's just no stress anymore.

WHAT IS YOUR BIGGEST MESSAGE TO WOMEN WHO HAVE NOT EXPERIENCED A CREATRIX® TRANSFORMATION?

I'd say to them to please recognise the negative chatter in your head and believe that Creatrix® can remove it. Have faith in the Transformologist® who tells you about it. Believe that it really is NOT "too good to be true". Let yourself go, immerse in the process and transform your life. Creatrix® works.

JOANNE (JO) BEECH, 49

I have four children and a granddaughter, and live with my partner and 10-year-old.

WHAT WERE THE THREE BIGGEST BLOCKS YOU USED CREATRIX® FOR?

Rejection, never feeling good enough, failure.

HOW LONG AGO DID YOU HAVE CREATRIX® ON THESE ISSUES?

February 2020.

WHAT ELSE HAD YOU TRIED PRIOR TO CREATRIX®?

Psychologists, counsellors, group therapy, self-help books, personal development books.

WHAT QUALIFICATIONS DID YOU HAVE WHEN YOU TRIED CREATRIX®?

Christian counsellor, beauty therapist, hospitality management.

PROFESSIONALLY, WHAT PROMPTED YOU TO SEEK OUT AN ALTERNATIVE TO THE METHODS YOU WERE USING?

I had previously had many major breakthroughs but still lived with anxiety, head chatter and no inner peace. I was helping others and felt like a fraud.

PERSONALLY, WHY DID YOU DECIDE YOU COULDN'T CONTINUE AS YOU WERE?

I knew there was more in life and I had a destiny to fulfill but I was sick to death of living with myself. I was committing all my energy to not being miserable.

WHO ELSE WOULD SUFFER IF THINGS STAYED THE SAME?

My children had suffered for 30 years. I'd gone through two divorces and was unhappy in another relationship. My 10-year-old son had cerebral palsy and needed more of me. I constantly struggled with suicidal thoughts.

IF YOU DIDN'T CHANGE, WHAT DID YOUR FUTURE LOOK LIKE?

Alone, miserable or even worse. It would rob my four children of their mother.

CRUNCH MOMENT – WHAT WAS THE DEFINING MOMENT THAT MADE YOU DECIDE TO HAVE CREATRIX®?

I found the web page looking for education to further help my clients and the words I read were like a baseball bat to my head, addressing everything I had ever struggled with and the freedom I had always dreamt of.

WHAT IS DIFFERENT NOW?

I am happy all the time. I have inner peace. I am not crying at the drop of a hat. I don't spend the day sleeping. I am able to parent with joy.

HOW HAS IT IMPACTED YOUR LOVED ONES?

I can now care for them instead of everyone else picking up the slack. Everyone is happy, together and excited for the future.

WHAT IS YOUR BIGGEST MESSAGE TO WOMEN WHO HAVE NOT EXPERIENCED A CREATRIX® TRANSFORMATION?

Be the reason you and your children, your grandchildren and all future generations can live without generational baggage; help them live the life they were created to live.

JULIE BRABY, 51

Widow with three children and I live with my son.

WHAT WERE THE THREE BIGGEST BLOCKS YOU USED CREATRIX® FOR?

I can't do it, keep the peace, never good enough.

HOW LONG AGO DID YOU HAVE CREATRIX® ON THESE ISSUES?

April 2020.

WHAT ELSE HAD YOU TRIED PRIOR TO CREATRIX®?

Tapping and counselling.

WHAT QUALIFICATIONS DID YOU HAVE WHEN YOU TRIED CREATRIX®?

Crystal healing practitioner; Reiki I and II.

PERSONALLY, WHY DID YOU DECIDE YOU COULDN'T CONTINUE AS YOU WERE?

It's been a pattern in my working career that I have felt overlooked for the actual contribution I was making, but didn't have the confidence to speak up or do anything to change it or make it better. I wasn't afraid to speak up on behalf of others, but when it came to me, I hated the thought of creating conflict, so would say nothing. I didn't feel good enough or deserving of being heard, paid more or treated better. I had a lack of self-worth, lack of confidence, was overweight and had no motivation to do anything about it. I was angry and resentful but felt hopeless about ever changing my situation. My self-confidence was lacking, so I constantly needed reassurance I was doing a good job and would get anxiety thinking I couldn't do my work.

What I wanted to do was have my own thing that I was passionate about that would have me jumping out of bed motivated, excited and able to earn an income. I wanted to work hard, for myself, not someone else. That's how I found Creatrix®. The bonus was I could get rid of my own limiting beliefs as part of the process and on an ongoing basis.

WHO ELSE WOULD SUFFER IF THINGS STAYED THE SAME?

I wasn't happy with my life and my kids weren't seeing the best version of their mother. I wasn't being the role model that I wanted to be for them, and this made me feel guilty.

IF YOU DIDN'T CHANGE, WHAT DID YOUR FUTURE LOOK LIKE?

I would have continued to be overweight, lack self-confidence and motivation, have no voice, be afraid to communicate in a calm way what I wanted/needed in work and personal situations.

Basically I would have been miserable and depressed about my lack of direction for my future.

CRUNCH MOMENT – WHAT WAS THE DEFINING MOMENT THAT MADE YOU DECIDE TO HAVE CREATRIX®?

I was having my first decent holiday after an extremely stressful and chaotic 18 months at work. Having the time off made me realise I needed to do something to get myself out of the current situation that was making me so unhappy.

I wanted fulfilment and happiness in my day and the only way I was going to get that was to take action. When I read about Creatrix®, it resonated immediately with me and I just knew it was what I wanted to experience and do. It was what I had been searching for.

WHAT IS DIFFERENT NOW?

I am so motivated now to exercise and do things to improve my life that I would easily have found an excuse to delay doing in the past. I have more confidence and am able to say what I need to say and believe in myself and my abilities.

HOW HAS IT IMPACTED YOUR LOVED ONES?

My children, family and friends have noticed how confident I have become and I'm a much happier person to be around. My success has motivated others to make changes in their lives.

WHAT IS YOUR BIGGEST MESSAGE TO WOMEN WHO HAVE NOT EXPERIENCED A CREATRIX® TRANSFORMATION?

Creatrix® has had the most profound impact on my life, for the better. I can't believe how powerful, yet simple, the process is to get lasting change from limiting beliefs or negative patterns holding you back from living your life to the fullest.

I have completely changed and it's so obvious for others to see they are reaching out to find out what I'm doing.

Everyone needs to know about Creatrix®.

KYLIE BONNOR, 38

Army wife married to Dave with three kids (two with special needs).

WHAT WERE THE THREE BIGGEST BLOCKS YOU USED CREATRIX® FOR?

Anger, exhaustion, and never feeling good enough as a mum, as a wife, as a daughter, and in my business.

HOW LONG AGO DID YOU HAVE CREATRIX® ON THESE ISSUES?

May 2017.

WHAT ELSE HAD YOU TRIED PRIOR TO CREATRIX®?

Many years of counselling, psychology, psychiatry, personal development, professional development, women's retreats, mindfulness-based stress reduction courses.

WHAT QUALIFICATIONS DID YOU HAVE WHEN YOU TRIED CREATRIX®?

I had spent the previous five years researching science and epigenetic medical info and journals and speaking with medical and science gurus trying to find answers to and heal my kids' genetic and other health issues. Maz's info on adults and epigenetic changes from Creatrix® really made me take notice (I'd known her for around 15 years at that point and had witnessed friends and colleagues have great results, and they'd encouraged me to try it simply to help me find my calm.)

PROFESSIONALLY, WHAT PROMPTED YOU TO SEEK OUT AN ALTERNATIVE TO THE METHODS YOU WERE USING?

Nothing was working so far. I was at an absolute breaking point after a few incredibly stressful years and I was looking for a change in career after moving a lot for so many years, always restarting my business every time we moved with Defence. When I did get a job, it really compromised my ethics and integrity. I lasted two days, hit absolutely rock bottom because if I'd ignored my values, what else was I willing to compromise on, and so decided if Creatrix® was supposed to be so great then maybe I needed to do it to help other women like me.

PERSONALLY, WHY DID YOU DECIDE YOU COULDN'T CONTINUE AS YOU WERE?

I didn't love myself and I couldn't live my life knowing I had compromised my integrity and values. I had only ever wanted to be a mum but by now I was HATING my kids and feeling like a constant failure in every department of my life. I didn't realise at the time just how close to breaking point I really was until after I'd had Creatrix® and an incident highlighted the Sliding Doors style of reality that I was on the path to.

With my work, I had overcome a million obstacles to get where I was but I still wasn't where I wanted to be because we moved all the time and I'd have to restart each time (in the era before online business was a big thing and our company wasn't really set up well for it at that stage), when it was good, I would maintain my customer service but that ate hugely into my profits with costs of postage taking a big percentage from my bottom line.

WHO ELSE WOULD SUFFER IF THINGS STAYED THE SAME?

My kids copped the worst of me. I remember they were so scared of me, I was like a Jekyll and Hyde mum yelling one minute then feeling guilty and trying to make up for it the next, but the anger would never leave me. I'd get them to school, then need all day to recover and prepare for the last few hours to get us through to bedtime and then take the rest of the evening till I went to bed trying to recover and supermum myself into the next episode of Groundhog Day. My husband missed out on the fun sexy wife he married because I was always tired trying to maintain and uphold the image I needed to portray so no one would discover how much of a hot mess I really was. My friends missed the person that always saw the bright side and made light of life and had lots of fun too.

IF YOU DIDN'T CHANGE, WHAT DID YOUR FUTURE LOOK LIKE?

I would have walked out and left my family permanently, thinking I was doing the best thing by them not to ruin their lives any further. I would have destroyed my family and myself either physically or emotionally in the process of trying to just survive as I had been.

CRUNCH MOMENT – WHAT WAS THE DEFINING MOMENT THAT MADE YOU DECIDE TO HAVE CREATRIX®?

The realisation that nothing had changed, I ran away from home for a month to try and recover and soothe my soul because I was at breaking point. I'd come back and Dave left again the next day for work so I landed with a thud. Things had gone along for another six weeks with life as I knew it and I was back at the breaking point, not refreshed or re-energised, always snapping at the kids and exhausted. I missed out on yet another job after the interviewer had asked about my personal life. I went to the doctor to ask for some antidepressants and she said I'd made it through so much so I should try and hang on just a bit longer to do a parenting course with her the following week and then we'd decide if I needed the drugs. The course was postponed a week, then cancelled, and I'd decided that this was my last chance and suddenly it wasn't an option, so Creatrix® became my last resort. I actually didn't realise at the time but I made no plans beyond the course, it really was a pinpoint of time in my life that I was doing the course and then I'd decide the next step so I'm ever so grateful I chose to go because my body and mind couldn't have continued living that life. If nothing changes, nothing changes, so I had to start the change process.

WHAT IS DIFFERENT NOW?

Personally: I'm not an angry mum anymore. I still have moments with children who press buttons or do silly things and I get angry, but it's fleeting and in the moment, and I recognise that it's childishness and usually fairly innocent or misguided as opposed to it being my kids' personal vendetta against me and my lacking abilities as a mum. I don't have anxiety anymore, which I never realised was a problem for me. If I feel anxious, I am really keenly aware of it and can deal with whatever is causing the anxiety in a really present and empowered way, which has made me more resilient as a result.

Professionally: I've saved other women and families like me from their desperate and often dark hole. I've helped women in Defence and emergency services not feel like failures in a system that really isn't family or mental health friendly. I've saved a woman's life and the ripple effect of that on her husband, children and colleagues saved a few more as well (that we know of). I've taught mothers to respect and trust their female intuition and understand their cycle and the awesomeness of their bodies. I've helped couples on the brink of collapse to understand each other and find neutral ground and reignite their relationships. Sometimes it's a bit of an ego trip but I'm grounded by my commitment to helping with the mission of 10 million hearts set free, and any woman I help makes another family's future brighter!

HOW HAS IT IMPACTED YOUR LOVED ONES?

The kids are really secure and know they are loved. As parents we discuss things more and aren't as black and white as we used to be, we think of the longer term picture rather than just the here and now, and are really open to learning and not caught up in the shitty dialogue that we aren't good enough parents. I don't hate my kids; I'm really proud of who they are. Even though they had a few rough years of me not at my best, they are strong, brave and resilient, and I can enjoy them and their crazy antics and love them unconditionally which feels like how it's supposed to, right at my core. I tell people about my journey though in the hope that it helps others not to feel too ashamed and not seek help if they need it.

WHAT IS YOUR BIGGEST MESSAGE TO WOMEN WHO HAVE NOT EXPERIENCED A CREATRIX® TRANSFORMATION?

If you're wondering if it could work for you, especially if you've tried everything else and nothing has, then I ask you, what have you got to lose? YOU might not need it to save your life, but maybe it could save your children from feeling the same way you did. Be their role model and begin to break the cycle, change the patterns and enjoy living life the way we were designed to live it. The worst thing would be that it doesn't work and nothing changes, in which case nothing will be different, but if it DOES work, the ripple effect is life-changing. And it's just way more enjoyable living life the way we were designed.

I love the saying "What would you do if you knew you could not fail?" I love asking women I meet this question in regards to Creatrix®. What would you do if Creatrix® changed your life?

KYLIE EVANS, 50

I have one son, one daughter and one grandson, and I share a house with a very good friend.

WHAT WERE THE THREE BIGGEST BLOCKS YOU USED CREATRIX® FOR?

I felt uneducated and frustrated. I hated this about myself.
I lacked confidence and self-esteem in a HUGE way.
I didn't think I would succeed in being successful at anything that really mattered.

HOW LONG AGO DID YOU HAVE CREATRIX® ON THESE ISSUES?

May 2020.

WHAT ELSE HAD YOU TRIED PRIOR TO CREATRIX®?

I saw a counsellor a few times and I saw a psychiatrist one time. It wasn't for me.

WHAT QUALIFICATIONS DID YOU HAVE WHEN YOU TRIED CREATRIX®?

I had NO qualifications at all. Nothing on a piece of legal paper anyway.

PERSONALLY, WHY DID YOU DECIDE YOU COULDN'T CONTINUE AS YOU WERE?

I knew I couldn't continue as I was for any longer because of the frustration of having so much love and passion inside of me that I wanted to help so many people that may have been hurting like I was. I wanted others to know somebody cared about them and understood how they may have been feeling. Not having the confidence to go beyond the REEF so to speak, as in the movie MOANA, drove me absolutely insane. The anxiety and frustration was killing me bit by bit every single day.

WHO ELSE WOULD SUFFER IF THINGS STAYED THE SAME?

Firstly, my ex partner suffered a lot. I blamed him for sooooo much, that I now know had a lot to do with how I felt about myself as a person, as a woman, and my insecurities of NOT feeling good about myself from my past. Sadly, he passed away so I will never get the chance to say sorry. My children definitely suffered; my crazy and insane outbursts of frustration and not feeling good enough were terrible. My dear friend, who has been trying his damnedest to help me build my confidence for the last 8 years. Everyone was suffering because of who I was and what I had been through in my past.

IF YOU DIDN'T CHANGE, WHAT DID YOUR FUTURE LOOK LIKE?

My future would have been extremely lonely. I was pushing all my loved ones away from me so I didn't continue to lash out at them with my crazy outbursts and hurt them. I was like Jekyll and Hyde at times. A very sad and lonely life was what was going to be served up for me if something didn't change for me ASAP.

CRUNCH MOMENT – WHAT WAS THE DEFINING MOMENT THAT MADE YOU DECIDE TO HAVE CREATRIX®?

Feeling so distant from my family who I love more than anything. Feeling like history was repeating itself as I was having crazy outbursts towards my friend. It was at this time I truly knew it was all about how I actually felt about myself. I just blamed everyone else for how I was feeling. Something had to change. I had to change. I had to get over all of my insecurities. I needed to change my way of thinking.

WHAT IS DIFFERENT NOW?

I look back at my life pre-Creatrix® and I can't believe how far I have come in such a short time. There is a HUGE outstanding difference in the way I think post-Creatrix®. I never really loved the person I was, I felt unloved, not wanted, unappreciated. I was soooo unhappy as a child and this just continued in me as an adult. NOW, after Creatrix®, I actually really love the person I am. I can't believe I had held onto those negative beliefs for all those years and let it rule my life until now. TODAY, I am so calm and happy. I really love the person, woman, mother, grandmother, friend I am today. Creatrix® has truly change my life in a way I cannot describe. It is truly magical and I feel like I am in a fairy tale life of happiness.

HOW HAS IT IMPACTED YOUR LOVED ONES?

My family get to have the happy fun loving, non-stressed out anxiety driven lunatic mother, grandmother, friend whom they love so much. I was always the mother that worried about every little thing. I wanted to make sure I was a FANTASTIC mother, wife, friend, grandmother, so much that it drove everyone insane. Since Creatrix® I am just the cool, calm and collected happy Kylie that everyone can enjoy hanging out with now. I am not the only WINNER from me having Creatrix®, my WHOLE family benefits from me having Creatrix®.

WHAT IS YOUR BIGGEST MESSAGE TO WOMEN WHO HAVE NOT EXPERIENCED A CREATRIX® TRANSFORMATION?

Since Creatrix® in May 2020 I look at life so differently. I know that this really is the start of me deciding to live, rather than just existing. Ohhhh boy there is a huge difference ladies, let me tell YOU.

Ladies, JUST DO IT. It WILL change your life FOREVER.

LEANNE BOYD, 56

I am married with three children and I care for my amazing 94-year-old mother.

WHAT WERE THE THREE BIGGEST BLOCKS YOU USED CREATRIX® FOR?

Betrayal was extremely hard for me to admit. During my life, betrayal was evident, but I could not see it for what it was. It ran deep within me, but I always mistook my feelings as resentment. No one likes to be betrayed.

Grief was my constant shadow as long as I could remember having said goodbye to many loved ones, including my father and sister. Fire destroyed our family home, my mother was left badly injured, and our most treasured possessions were gone. Suicide and cancer took four of my best friends. I often wondered why I had to endure this level of unbearable sadness.

As the youngest of six children, I grew up feeling judged and not good enough. I was the baby, seen and not heard. Growing up, these feelings continued. I could never achieve what I wanted because everyone seemed better than me.

HOW LONG AGO DID YOU HAVE CREATRIX® ON THESE ISSUES?

November 2013.

WHAT ELSE HAD YOU TRIED PRIOR TO CREATRIX®?

I had tried NLP for a short time with no results. Nothing seemed to change. I read many self-help books, seeking help for anxiety and depression. Acupuncture for anxiety gave relief short-term.

WHAT QUALIFICATIONS DID YOU HAVE WHEN YOU TRIED CREATRIX®?

I had no formal qualifications when I first tried Creatrix®. I had had aspirations for almost two decades of practicing natural medicine. Not having completed my senior education at school, I thought that I would never be accepted into a college.

PERSONALLY, WHY DID YOU DECIDE YOU COULDN'T CONTINUE AS YOU WERE?

Prior to Creatrix®, I felt like second-best, no matter what I did. The sad little girl who was never listened to haunted me. I couldn't be free until she was. Everyone was confident and happy, and I was not! I wanted to be courageous but instead I was angry, depressed and lonely. I was my own prisoner. Peace, serenity and calmness eluded me for an endlessly chattering mind.

I wanted to change and turn my years of fear and self-doubt into something positive and help other women who had been through silent sadness too.

WHO ELSE WOULD SUFFER IF THINGS STAYED THE SAME?

Total despair seeped into my relationship with my husband, our children and friends. I didn't want my children to remember growing up with a sad, broken mother who was always crying and never happy. I wasn't capable of giving motherly love to them. I was constantly irrational, angry and resentful. Trapped inside lonely sorrow and low self-esteem, I became needy and friends never stayed long.

IF YOU DIDN'T CHANGE, WHAT DID YOUR FUTURE LOOK LIKE?

I was destined for lifelong regret in an unfulfilled life. I wasn't the mum, wife, friend I wanted to be, and I certainly would never have become the natural healer I am today. Sadness and anxiety would be in control.

CRUNCH MOMENT – WHAT WAS THE DEFINING MOMENT THAT MADE YOU DECIDE TO HAVE CREATRIX®?

On New Year's Day 2012, I was watching the ocean waves roll in as my children played on the beach without me. I recalled all the ones I loved who had left this world. Their faces in my thoughts made me realise how I was wasting time in my life when their life had been cut short. I was still here, and they were not. These souls inspired me to gather myself together the best way I could to help other women pick up their life too.

I began to run motivational events for women. At one event, I met Maz Schirmer, founder of Creatrix®. This was a pivotal moment in my journey to where I am today.

WHAT IS DIFFERENT NOW?

My blissful heart is completely open to all that comes my way. I truly believe that anything is possible, and now, with my knowledge and experience, I have helped other women achieve great things too and find their own version of personal freedom, health and vitality.

I am totally free to be me! Post-Creatrix®, everything seemed possible! I enrolled for study at 49 years of age after 34 years away from formal education. I am now a naturopath, clinical reflexologist, Creatrix® Transformologist®, leadership coach and mentor. I have emotional freedom for a limitless life. I can achieve anything I want.

HOW HAS IT IMPACTED YOUR LOVED ONES?

Everyone noticed a change in me. My husband, Scott, said he missed the woman he first met. Where had she gone? Now my smile is back, and we love spending quality time together. I encourage my children to be brave and take every opportunity they can, and they do. This would not be the case if they were all still living with the old me.

WHAT IS YOUR BIGGEST MESSAGE TO WOMEN WHO HAVE NOT EXPERIENCED A CREATRIX® TRANSFORMATION?

Creatrix® is liberating! Just do it!
Don't allow fear, doubt and stress to maim your life. Our mind and body are connected and if you choose to allow past hurts to influence your life, then in a deterministic way, your body may respond with poor well-being.

You MUST put your own oxygen mask on first to thrive. Make your goal meaningful change. As a woman, your heart holds the best vision and purpose for your life so look within. Be present with love and laugh with gratitude.

LINDA DE VRIES, 40

Living together with my partner and our two kids.

___

WHAT WERE THE THREE BIGGEST BLOCKS YOU USED CREATRIX® FOR?

When I started the course there was a lot of unrest, tension, feeling busy, stressed and hunted in my life.
If I would be on my own in the future, I would not accomplish anything and that would feel like failure.
If I went for my dream for having a third child, I would lose my partner.

HOW LONG AGO DID YOU HAVE CREATRIX® ON THESE ISSUES?

May 2017.

WHAT ELSE HAD YOU TRIED PRIOR TO CREATRIX®?

Outplacement program with a psychologist, haptonomy, counselling, foot reflexology massage, social work.

WHAT QUALIFICATIONS DID YOU HAVE WHEN YOU TRIED CREATRIX®?

Elementary teacher and special education teacher, naturopathic worker.

PROFESSIONALLY, WHAT PROMPTED YOU TO SEEK OUT AN ALTERNATIVE TO THE METHODS YOU WERE USING?

I was coaching people to get healthy and to build their own business. I noticed that when my help ended, it was very difficult for them to stay on track. My own business was getting harder at that point. After working hard and keeping on going, I was searching for help. At that point I discovered Creatrix®, my missing piece. It is so important that you first have a strong mind and clean up the past before anything else!

PERSONALLY, WHY DID YOU DECIDE YOU COULDN'T CONTINUE AS YOU WERE?

I couldn't continue as I was. After being a teacher for 14 years and coaching for two years, I was searching for a job I could really get satisfaction from. I wanted to have a job where I could really make change and I could fully stand behind. To make my own choices, help other women and have flexible work conditions.

WHO ELSE WOULD SUFFER IF THINGS STAYED THE SAME?

There was a lot of unrest, tension, feeling busy, stressed and hunted in my life. I wanted to do everything perfectly. The kids had to look good, eat well and be on time for school. At the moment of leaving for school, I was frustrated and feeling stressed and that was unpleasant for my kids.

I was angry at my partner because he didn't have that big wish for a third child. It was a negative circle to break. I was scared to lose my partner when I would truly be myself so I couldn't be the woman he met 14 years ago.

IF YOU DIDN'T CHANGE, WHAT DID YOUR FUTURE LOOK LIKE?

My kids would have a mum that wasn't really herself and truly happy, a mum that had a short fuse and was sad, angry and in a hurry.

There would be too much grief by losing our third child by a miscarriage. I couldn't work for my business, and I was very sad and angry at my partner.

CRUNCH MOMENT – WHAT WAS THE DEFINING MOMENT THAT MADE YOU DECIDE TO HAVE CREATRIX®?

I could choose to do a breakthrough for myself or to do the course, which includes my own breakthrough. I was searching for both: be the best me and have a job that would fit with my family and to really contribute to the world. I decided to go for it!

Two years later... six weeks after my miscarriage, weeks of crying a lot and having a hard time, I felt I would like to go on with my life. To enjoy the life I had, my lovely partner, our wonderful kids and my beautiful business. I didn't see a way to go on with my life. There was too much grief, anger and feeling of failing. The only way to get myself together was to have Creatrix®.

WHAT IS DIFFERENT NOW?

It helped me so much. After the course, I was so much more relaxed. The relationship with my kids is better, more cuddles from my son who doesn't like to cuddle much.

We have less arguments and more love. I finally found the best job ever. It was like coming home, so interesting, helpful for myself and for so many other women!!

Two years later, I could go on with my life. I will never forget the loss of our third child. There can be a tear once in a while; our little one has a special place in my heart. And I feel stronger and like I am being the best version of myself. So I can go on with my life, enjoy our family and my job!

HOW HAS IT IMPACTED YOUR LOVED ONES?

There is more peace in our home, less arguments. The kids are growing up with a supportive mom. I can stay calm when they have their issues. I help them but I don't feel responsible for everything. Our family is closer now. Me and my partner can talk better when there are some difficulties. Friends and family see I'm happier now and that I can be the real me.

WHAT IS YOUR BIGGEST MESSAGE TO WOMEN WHO HAVE NOT EXPERIENCED A CREATRIX® TRANSFORMATION?

I wish every woman could experience their own Creatrix® breakthrough; that you can finally be the real you; that you can break the cycle and pattern for your children and grandchildren; that you can give your grief a place and still have your own beautiful memories; that you can see what you learned from the more difficult parts of your life and that it's now time to look to the future and enjoy the moment!

LOUISE BONNER, 55

I have been married for 30 years. Mother of three beautiful adult daughters.

WHAT WERE THE THREE BIGGEST BLOCKS YOU USED CREATRIX® FOR?

The three biggest blocks I have used Creatrix® for were limiting beliefs. I was feeling stuck at times and I had a lack of self-belief.

HOW LONG AGO DID YOU HAVE CREATRIX® ON THESE ISSUES?

April 2020.

WHAT ELSE HAD YOU TRIED PRIOR TO CREATRIX®?

A lot of personal development.

WHAT QUALIFICATIONS DID YOU HAVE WHEN YOU TRIED CREATRIX®?

Business owner and putting into practice many personal development concepts.

PERSONALLY, WHY DID YOU DECIDE YOU COULDN'T CONTINUE AS YOU WERE?

I have studied personal development for many years. This was introduced to me through my job. It was called "training" back then. It was with a group of work colleagues and I absolutely thrived off it. It was one specific day in time that opened my mind to the possibilities and the potential of what life can be like when the correct practices are taught and put into place. Though information, methods and technique are wonderful tools to have, there was a missing piece.

Basically, I knew there was more to me and that I was keen to tap into that space. I wanted to live life the best way I could. I wanted to enjoy the beauty of it, and it was important to me to make a difference in other people's lives. This can be done in so many ways, yet to do this I needed to be the best I could be so working on myself and being real was important.

WHO ELSE WOULD SUFFER IF THINGS STAYED THE SAME?

I was quietly suffering from not knowing how to clear the root cause that was coming from my subconscious mind. When we feel more contented, it shows up in so many ways.

IF YOU DIDN'T CHANGE, WHAT DID YOUR FUTURE LOOK LIKE?

My future me would be limited. I wanted my future to be more than that.

CRUNCH MOMENT – WHAT WAS THE DEFINING MOMENT THAT MADE YOU DECIDE TO HAVE CREATRIX®?

I had never heard of Creatrix® Transformology®. Ironically, I was not looking for it, yet subconsciously it was a different story.

The morning I heard Maz Schirmer speaking about it, I honestly wanted to reject it at first, because I was involved in other business obligations. I was thinking, "I don't have the time and funds to spend any more on this stuff!"

Her words just continued to "ring in my ears". I switched it off and tried to forget about it, but it did not want to leave my conscious mind.

I put in a call to find out more. The following week I left for a business trip overseas and thought to myself, "If I continue to think about this, I will need to do something about it." Five weeks later the decision was made. I invested in me!

WHAT IS DIFFERENT NOW?

Me. I am still learning and growing from this and will continue to do so for a long time yet. Generally, I feel more self-confident and calmer. I am also more aware and I don't hang on to negativity for too long. I have the ability to shake things off and if it continues to bother me, Creatrix® is there.

Having Creatrix® available removes any excuses from getting your nonsense sorted. It is there to clear out our negative blocks and beliefs.

There is no greater feeling than to provide freedom, peace of mind and to help set female hearts free. This is priceless.

HOW HAS IT IMPACTED YOUR LOVED ONES?

When mama bear is happy, so is her family. When boss lady is calmer, so is her team. Basically, that is what has happened. You will hear about the ripple effect and that is precisely what it is. Living your best self through ups and downs.

WHAT IS YOUR BIGGEST MESSAGE TO WOMEN WHO HAVE NOT EXPERIENCED A CREATRIX® TRANSFORMATION?

If you feel like you need help and it has been something that you have not been able to manage or bothers you or your life, time is ticking by. You either choose to live with it or, if you are serious about doing something about it, there is Creatrix®.

Creatrix® can give you the inner confidence that is "gold" when "life is happening" and things aren't going so well. If you invest in yourself you will be able to get through anything, no matter what.

Set yourself free.

MAGALI GENDRE, 42

I live with my partner and my three boys. I am French and have been living in Australia for over nine years now.

WHAT WERE THE THREE BIGGEST BLOCKS YOU USED CREATRIX® FOR?

The three biggest blocks I have used Creatrix® for were being stressed, guilty and angry.

HOW LONG AGO DID YOU HAVE CREATRIX® ON THESE ISSUES?

October 2015.

WHAT ELSE HAD YOU TRIED PRIOR TO CREATRIX®?

NLP coach, parenting coach, psychologist, reading books.

WHAT QUALIFICATIONS DID YOU HAVE WHEN YOU TRIED CREATRIX®?

Executive coach (with a little bit of use of NLP).

PROFESSIONALLY, WHAT PROMPTED YOU TO SEEK OUT AN ALTERNATIVE TO THE METHODS YOU WERE USING?

I had had enough of who I was. It was getting worse and worse. It really hurt me inside always being stressed, guilty and angry. Nothing that I would try would work for long. I was exhausted. And I know that I would not have been able to cope long staying like that. I was not sleeping well. I was not able to think clearly when I worked or at home. I was lacking energy. I was flat.

PERSONALLY, WHY DID YOU DECIDE YOU COULDN'T CONTINUE AS YOU WERE?

I decided that I couldn't continue because I was unhappy. My days looked like Groundhog Day and it was getting worse. I was exhausted. I did know deep inside of me that I was the problem and that I needed help to help myself. I started to react violently to my son's tantrums. It was not acceptable at all for me. I was becoming dangerous for him. So I needed to change.

WHO ELSE WOULD SUFFER IF THINGS STAYED THE SAME?

My kids had an angry yelling mum, always busy and stressed. And I was guilty of not just being with them. My youngest son was having tantrums, which were about not being able to manage and express his emotions. I did know that by helping me I would be able to help him. It was like he was trying to help me to express that anger. I was worried that if I continued, he would suffer with unhealthy behaviours all his life. His older brother would let him have the game or anything he was after so he would stay quiet. With any conflicts, they knew it would end up in tantrums and then I would get upset. As they wanted me to stay calm, they would make sure he would be getting what he wanted.

IF YOU DIDN'T CHANGE, WHAT DID YOUR FUTURE LOOK LIKE?

I would have damaged my kids more. It was getting worse as months passed. I would have left them so that the house would have been happier and calmer. I would have decided to see them less and less. I would have been stuck at work more often just to avoid time with them. My partner would have left me as I was not able to improve and I was less and less with them. I was a bad mum. I was not happy. It was getting heavier.

CRUNCH MOMENT – WHAT WAS THE DEFINING MOMENT THAT MADE YOU DECIDE TO HAVE CREATRIX®?

It was a Saturday morning, the start of the weekend. The weekend is meant to be the time for kids and for the family. And here it started from the first couple of hours of the day. My son wanted some biscuits. I said no as he had had breakfast earlier on. He was not happy with that response and started a tantrum. He started to yell and kicked me with his foot. I could not stay calm. I went off yelling as well and trying to catch him. He would not stop yelling. I had to go out of the house to not hear him. I could not stand it anymore. I was in tears. I went and attended a personal development speaking event where it was about angry mums. Creatrix® was used as the missing piece in order to transform yourself. I've never looked back.

WHAT IS DIFFERENT NOW?

I am not triggered anymore by the kids. I have stopped yelling. I do not feel that anger in me anymore. They are no angels and they are doing everyday things that I need to respond to, but I am not reacting anymore to it in anger. I am able to respond and be firm, yet still calm and patient. I am able to set boundaries for myself and for them in a healthy way. I have a REAL connection with my son who used to have tantrums. Our relationship has changed for the better. I have been able to change my parenting and I can help my kids to the best of my abilities.

I do not feel guilty anymore to be a working mum. I have long days where I am passionate about what I do, and it is okay. When I am with them, I can connect with them and be with them. A happy mum, who is okay with her choices, is all they need.

The tantrums have stopped by themselves. I was not getting triggered anymore. It was very strange at first as I could not feel anything inside myself. It was completely gone. I can see clearly what I want and what I do not want. I do not feel stressed anymore. I am so happy with my life.

HOW HAS IT IMPACTED YOUR LOVED ONES?

My youngest son stopped his tantrums not long after. It had a big impact on my kids' behaviour. I am closer than ever to my kids. I am able to discuss things with them now. I am able to let them explain what is happening for them and I am not overreacting to what they are doing. Our family is a lot calmer and happier. The saying "Happy mum = happy kids" is so real and true. I am a cool, calm and confident mum now, at peace with myself and them.

WHAT IS YOUR BIGGEST MESSAGE TO WOMEN WHO HAVE NOT EXPERIENCED A CREATRIX® TRANSFORMATION?

Every mum should be able to be set free as it is possible so easily now. A happy mum leads to happy kids. It has a ripple effect on their family, their friends, their colleagues, and the community around them. Those mums can rise and shine. They can be themselves. Imagine if all mums in the world are set free. It would have an impact on the world.

MARTIENE VAN DIS, 52

I live alone with my son and our dog.

WHAT WERE THE THREE BIGGEST BLOCKS YOU USED CREATRIX® FOR?

I am not good enough, I do not matter, I do not belong here.

HOW LONG AGO DID YOU HAVE CREATRIX® ON THESE ISSUES?

May 2018.

WHAT ELSE HAD YOU TRIED PRIOR TO CREATRIX®?

Mindfulness, coaching, reading self-help books, sports, dieting, yoga.

WHAT QUALIFICATIONS DID YOU HAVE WHEN YOU TRIED CREATRIX®?

Human Resources professional, trainer, team coach.

PERSONALLY, WHY DID YOU DECIDE YOU COULDN'T CONTINUE AS YOU WERE?

I already felt too long restless and alone. I was more in my head than in my heart and soul. I wished to be grounded and connected. I wanted to let go of my insecurities.

WHO ELSE WOULD SUFFER IF THINGS STAYED THE SAME?

My son of 10 years old. I did not want him to grow up with the same issues and with a yelling mum with mood swings.

IF YOU DIDN'T CHANGE, WHAT DID YOUR FUTURE LOOK LIKE?

I would always feel not good enough, I would be lonely, I would always be questioning myself. I would feel like a bad mom who had a lot of mood swings. I would punish myself mentally and let myself down, I would hate myself and tell myself that it was all because of me. I would not be able to give my son a loving and warm environment.

CRUNCH MOMENT – WHAT WAS THE DEFINING MOMENT THAT MADE YOU DECIDE TO HAVE CREATRIX®?

I just had a nasty argument with my son where I was treating him unfairly and I heard my inner voice questioning myself again and I was so tired and fed up that I decided I had to take responsibility and change this forever.

WHAT IS DIFFERENT NOW?

I feel good enough and worthy. My son tells me now what he likes and dislikes in my actions towards him, and I can hear him in the moment, think about it, talk with him about it, and show I can do it differently. In meetings/groups I can talk freely and easily about all issues even if I get emotionally involved.

HOW HAS IT IMPACTED YOUR LOVED ONES?

They can be themselves around me and we accept one another with lots of love and laughter, discussions and curiosity.

WHAT IS YOUR BIGGEST MESSAGE TO WOMEN WHO HAVE NOT EXPERIENCED A CREATRIX® TRANSFORMATION?

If you love yourself and the ones around you, then take your responsibility and break your patterns in order to become your true self, the role model you are meant to be. It brings so much peace upon you and the ones around you. And it stops the patterns being continued in your bloodline forever.

MONIQUE LIGTHART-HAUWERT, 42

I'm happily married with my husband and together we have two beautiful sons.

WHAT WERE THE THREE BIGGEST BLOCKS YOU USED CREATRIX® FOR?

I feel not worthy.
Fear to fail.
Fear of rejection.

HOW LONG AGO DID YOU HAVE CREATRIX® ON THESE ISSUES?

September 2019.

WHAT ELSE HAD YOU TRIED PRIOR TO CREATRIX®?

I have had personal coaching for six months, and I followed a coach training for three years. I have done various coach studies, Family Constellations and online courses. And I read a lot of self-help books.

WHAT QUALIFICATIONS DID YOU HAVE WHEN YOU TRIED CREATRIX®?

I am an accredited coach professional for ambitious, busy moms at my companies Unique.Mom and Women's Transformation Expert.

PROFESSIONALLY, WHAT PROMPTED YOU TO SEEK OUT AN ALTERNATIVE TO THE METHODS YOU WERE USING?

Professionally, I knew that my coaching methods and approaches were good, but there was always a missing piece. I had the feeling that I just tipped the top of the iceberg and that it was never really lasting. And that frustrated me and gave me the feeling that what I did wasn't good enough.

PERSONALLY, WHY DID YOU DECIDE YOU COULDN'T CONTINUE AS YOU WERE?

Personally, I decided that I couldn't continue my life the way it was because I had the feeling I lived on the handbrake. I always had the feeling that some things were holding me back. And I knew deep inside that I had so much more to give. That I could enjoy life so much more than I did. And that I could be a better mom and be more relaxed than I was as a woman and as a mom.

I also wanted to give my sons a great model by living by example. I wanted to show them that you can live the life you want. To be free, without boundaries and limited beliefs. There was also a family pattern in the women's line that I felt it was my assignment to break; to stop that pattern from going on another generation.

And besides my personal issues, I always have the motto that YOU and YOU ONLY are responsible for your life. And that IF you want to change it, you have to do it YOURSELF. Take the first step. Even if it scares the hell out of you. Because that's the moment something is really going to change in your life. For the better!

I made a lot of steps already, but there was still that feeling inside. Until I found Creatrix® and jumped on the course.

WHO ELSE WOULD SUFFER IF THINGS STAYED THE SAME?

I was not completely myself and not living my life fully so it would hurt everyone in my life. Because sometimes life frustrated me; I wasn't feeling good about myself, I was not happy with myself and my life, and therefore I was not kind to myself and everyone else around me. My kids especially would have suffered because I wasn't the best mom in the world for them. And I didn't want them to grow up and feel not happy with themselves either because of me or the way I lived.

My husband would have suffered because I was not the happy, enthusiastic, free woman I could be. Just like my family and friends. And of course, the women out there for whom I have my companies Unique.Mom and Women's Transformation Expert.

IF YOU DIDN'T CHANGE, WHAT DID YOUR FUTURE LOOK LIKE?

When I didn't change a thing, I would always have had the feeling, 'Is this really it? Is this what my life should look like?' Because deep down I knew it wasn't. I always would have asked myself what my life would have looked like if I had the power and belief to live my own life. And I would have searched forever for the key to internal peace.

CRUNCH MOMENT – WHAT WAS THE DEFINING MOMENT THAT MADE YOU DECIDE TO HAVE CREATRIX®?

The defining moment when I decide to sign up for the Creatrix® Transformology® course came after Creatrix® crossed my life a number of times. And that was a kind of sign for me that I had to do something with it. When I looked into Creatrix® on the Internet, I felt the itches in my belly every time I read about it. That together with my wish to help myself and the women in my company more effectively made me decide to do the Creatrix® Transformologist® course in The Netherlands.

WHAT IS DIFFERENT NOW?

The difference in my life now is that I am much more relaxed with myself and my kids. I'm more confident in who I am and the things I do. My downs are less deep and shorter. I recognise my patterns earlier.

I am so much more aware of myself and my reflection on my kids, my family and the world. I smile more and enjoy life so much more. I live more freely and openly.
I really live my life more to my fullest potential!

And when I see and feel there is something I have to work on, I know what to do! I ask for a Creatrix® session to break the pattern and work on the issue.

I also learned so much more about being a woman and how our bodies and hormones impact our lives, which meant that I am more kind to myself because I recognise the phase in my period and react to my needs.

HOW HAS IT IMPACTED YOUR LOVED ONES?

We were always a happy family and still are. But being more present as a mom, as a wife, and being more confident as a woman makes me more attractive in a positive way. I respect my own boundaries so much more, which has a positive effect on my family. I don't explode anymore because my kids or my husband aren't crossing my boundaries, because they are so much clearer. I am also a great example for my kids more than ever. A real role model!

So, it had, and still has, a great impact on my loved ones and that makes me proud and incredibly happy.

And that is why I am convinced that I will help a whole lot of woman with Unique.Mom, Women's Transformation Expert and Creatrix® and create a ripple effect for a lot of women and families and children.

WHAT IS YOUR BIGGEST MESSAGE TO WOMEN WHO HAVE NOT EXPERIENCED A CREATRIX® TRANSFORMATION?

My biggest message is that I think every woman needs to break the patterns. Not only for themselves but also for their kids, grandkids and so on. You are a role model! Be aware of that.

Creatrix® is the greatest gift you can give yourself. Break free from the negative patterns, the limited beliefs and the negative voice in your head, that little gremlin who is always waiting for the moment to keep you small and feel miserable.

When you get rid of these patterns, you find out that you are so much more powerful than you think you are. You will see life in a much brighter, clearer and happier way. You will find your true self and come home to yourself.

The only one who can change your life is YOU. It's your responsibility. And I think taking the responsibility for your own life is the greatest gift you can give yourself, and your children, grandchildren, etc. So break free and live free. And be a great example for the ones around you!

The tagline of Unique.Mom is "Be your own Unique self, and shine!"

NATALIE ANNE MURRAY, 50

I was widowed at 35 years old and I've been married to my second husband for 10 years. I never had children of my own, but I raised my two step-children full-time with my late husband, and I have four step-grandsons.

WHAT WERE THE THREE BIGGEST BLOCKS YOU USED CREATRIX® FOR?

I used to struggle with an obsessive need for approval, had a huge fear of being judged or rejected, and carried a lot of guilt about making bad relationship choices, being an angry mother, and for not living up to my potential.

HOW LONG AGO DID YOU HAVE CREATRIX® ON THESE ISSUES?

May 2016.

WHAT ELSE HAD YOU TRIED PRIOR TO CREATRIX®?

Before Creatrix®, I had tried inner child work, kinesiology, Emotional Freedom Technique, Family Systems therapy, and counselling.

WHAT QUALIFICATIONS DID YOU HAVE WHEN YOU TRIED CREATRIX®?

My professional background is as a Registered Mental Health Nurse, specialist trauma and abuse counsellor, and addiction and co-dependency recovery mentor.

PROFESSIONALLY, WHAT PROMPTED YOU TO SEEK OUT AN ALTERNATIVE TO THE METHODS YOU WERE USING?

I had done so much work on myself but still felt like I was faking my confidence personally and professionally and that felt soul-destroying.

PERSONALLY, WHY DID YOU DECIDE YOU COULDN'T CONTINUE AS YOU WERE?

When I was 45 years old, I burnt out physically, emotionally, and spiritually by giving too much of myself to try and prove my worth. I realised I'd been living for other people, and I couldn't waste my time and talents anymore. I wanted to be successful just by being me, but my fears and insecurities held me back.

WHO ELSE WOULD SUFFER IF THINGS STAYED THE SAME?

My husband suffered because I was always anxious and feeling bad about myself and I blamed him and our relationship for my unhappiness. I hid who I really was from my family and isolated myself so all the women I was born to serve missed out on my help.

IF YOU DIDN'T CHANGE, WHAT DID YOUR FUTURE LOOK LIKE?

If I hadn't decided to change, my marriage would be over, and I would have pushed my family and friends away. I would live a lonely life in an unfulfilling job I hated and stuff down my pain with food. I wouldn't be living my purpose and I would be filled with regrets.

CRUNCH MOMENT – WHAT WAS THE DEFINING MOMENT THAT MADE YOU DECIDE TO HAVE CREATRIX®?

My turning point came when I started an online business and was paralysed by the thought of being seen on social media. When I did my first Facebook Live, I was overcome with fear and toxic shame, and I cried in bed for days. I knew then my issues ran deep and that I would never move forward unless I dealt with them. I was completely over it all and was prepared to do whatever it took to break free from my suffering.

WHAT IS DIFFERENT NOW?

Now I no longer feel like life is a struggle. My mind is quiet and positive, and my body is free from emotional pain and angst. I feel like a woman of integrity who lives true to herself, and I don't worry anymore about what other people think of me, which is such a relief. I'm confidently moving forward in my business and when challenges arise, I take responsibility for myself and solve the problem quickly and move on.

HOW HAS IT IMPACTED YOUR LOVED ONES?

My husband and I get on really well and rarely fight anymore. My kids and family now know the real me and we're closer than ever before. I also have a lot more friends and feel confident to just be me with everyone. Most importantly, my stepdaughter has been influenced by my changes, and she's choosing to change for the better too, which feels amazing.

WHAT IS YOUR BIGGEST MESSAGE TO WOMEN WHO HAVE NOT EXPERIENCED A CREATRIX® TRANSFORMATION?

I know it can be challenging to make the decision to transform yourself and your life. On the one hand, it feels liberating and exciting, but on the other hand, it feels scary to face the unknown. My biggest fear was, Who would I be without my issues? but the truth was I was very, very unhappy so it made no sense to keep holding on to them.

If you too feel in your gut that you were born to be a changemaker, I strongly encourage you to take a leap of faith, invest in yourself, and become a true role model for future generations. Breaking the cycle of disempowerment in your family is the most profound and important choice you will ever make in your lifetime, and it's so simple and easy that you will wonder why you waited for so long!

You deserve to be free from suffering and struggle.

You deserve to just be you.

RAE SKINNER, 51

Happily married 30-plus years with two adult children and two grandchildren

WHAT WERE THE THREE BIGGEST BLOCKS YOU USED CREATRIX® FOR?

Anxiety. Depression. I'm not good enough.

HOW LONG AGO DID YOU HAVE CREATRIX® ON THESE ISSUES?

March 2017.

WHAT ELSE HAD YOU TRIED PRIOR TO CREATRIX®?

Counselling, psychology, various spiritual modalities, NLP, Time Line Therapy.

WHAT QUALIFICATIONS DID YOU HAVE WHEN YOU TRIED CREATRIX®?

Grief loss counsellor and life/relationship coach.

PROFESSIONALLY, WHAT PROMPTED YOU TO SEEK OUT AN ALTERNATIVE TO THE METHODS YOU WERE USING?

Various losses (including a child) led me into counselling and wanting to help women recover from their own losses, but it hurt too much. So I became a life coach, until I realised that I couldn't help anyone unless I got help for myself first. Creatrix® changed all that for me.

PERSONALLY, WHY DID YOU DECIDE YOU COULDN'T CONTINUE AS YOU WERE?

I was at my wits' end. Nothing else had worked long-term, and a female-specific process, addressing epigenetic and chronic emotional issues held in the unconscious mind, just seemed to make sense. I was a shotgun baby that spent her life believing she should have never existed. I became a mum at 22 and that became my purpose. When my mothering days ended, I felt lost. I didn't know who I was or what I wanted, I just existed, and I didn't want live anymore like that.

WHO ELSE WOULD SUFFER IF THINGS STAYED THE SAME?

My husband had a sad wife he couldn't fix or understand. My kids had a mum who was overemotional and reactive. My grandchildren would have been robbed of a playful, joyous nan.

IF YOU DIDN'T CHANGE, WHAT DID YOUR FUTURE LOOK LIKE?

I don't think I'd be here to comment.

CRUNCH MOMENT – WHAT WAS THE DEFINING MOMENT THAT MADE YOU DECIDE TO HAVE CREATRIX®?

Waking up in hospital after an overdose five years prior and seeing what that did to my family. I vowed to not give up on myself again and was determined to find a solution.

WHAT IS DIFFERENT NOW?

Life is like night and day now. I love and respect myself and my life fully now. I have passion and purpose, running a successful business and doing what's right for me, without anything holding me back from doing the things I want to. Totally amazing!

HOW HAS IT IMPACTED YOUR LOVED ONES?

My family is so much happier, calmer and connected now. My eldest son is a great father. My youngest son has improved his own life and he is also flourishing. And my husband's business is thriving also.

WHAT IS YOUR BIGGEST MESSAGE TO WOMEN WHO HAVE NOT EXPERIENCED A CREATRIX® TRANSFORMATION?

Don't hesitate! JUST DO IT! Honestly, there is no price you can put on quality of life and the ripple effect that will have on everyone around you, improving business success and chances at love. It's priceless!

REZZA CUSTODIO-SORIANO, 46

Married quite late in life at age 39, together for seven years since. Hubby and I have no kids yet and are living with our five adopted kitties.

WHAT WERE THE THREE BIGGEST BLOCKS YOU USED CREATRIX® FOR?

I'm not confident about my skills as an NLP life coach. I'm poor – I lacked the feeling and thinking of abundance, tended to undervalue myself.

Anger – seething anger towards a close family member for many things, being self-centred, greedy and desperate for money; blaming them for making my family member sick with Stage 4 cancer.

HOW LONG AGO DID YOU HAVE CREATRIX® ON THESE ISSUES?

June 2017.

WHAT ELSE HAD YOU TRIED PRIOR TO CREATRIX®?

Theta healing, NLP, and prayers.

WHAT QUALIFICATIONS DID YOU HAVE WHEN YOU TRIED CREATRIX®?

Christian counselling (15 years).
NLP practitioner classic and new code (six years).

PROFESSIONALLY, WHAT PROMPTED YOU TO SEEK OUT AN ALTERNATIVE TO THE METHODS YOU WERE USING?

I felt the constraint and limitation of doing NLP online. Since I didn't have a physical office, it was a logistical challenge to conduct sessions face-to-face. Plus, I wasn't absolutely satisfied with the methods I had, because of that nagging thought that I had clients whose issues weren't completely resolved or would just come back.

After being a professional life coach for six years, I didn't have the drive nor confidence to come out and declare my profession and business to the world. I was just relying on working in tandem with my husband, and he was the key driver in promoting our coaching business. My career had also taken a backseat because I made a conscious effort to *NOT* outshine my husband. In the process, I had become more hidden, making my own career languish, while my husband continually made his presence and profession known. I would rationalise and tell myself, "It's okay, he needs the attention and the growth more now." But deep inside I was feeling short-changed and resentful. I just KNEW I was meant for something greater, something bigger, something more KICK-A**, if I may say so. But I kept on self-sabotaging, postponing, delaying.

I was tagged by a friend on Facebook, and it was about something I've never heard before: Creatrix®. The moment I read through the Institute of Women International website, and watched Maz's videos, I got goosebumps. At the same time, I experienced a sudden flashback to a vision I had back in 2010: I was standing on an auditorium stage, delivering something inspiring to hundreds of women. Back then it was bewildering and it didn't make sense because I was in a totally different career. So while I was reading through the IOWI website, it felt like the universe was suddenly smiling at me, like it was finally presenting to me the missing piece in creating a purposeful and meaningful career in transforming the lives of women. It felt like a voice inside whispered, "Finally, you know what you need to do."

PERSONALLY, WHY DID YOU DECIDE YOU COULDN'T CONTINUE AS YOU WERE?

In 2017, I was carrying so much hate, anger and resentment in my life at that time. In January 2017, we discovered my dad was dying of Stage 4 cancer (type of cancer unknown). And I felt so angry at a family member because I truly felt and believed at that time that they were the cause of his sudden and mysterious illness, with all the mental, physical stress and verbal abuse they were hurling at him daily. This was compounded by other factors. I couldn't report to work at all because I was looking after my dad at the hospital full-time, buying his medicines and comforting him. I couldn't bring myself to attend prayer meetings nor practice life coaching, because I felt so disconnected trying to keep things together for the family.

WHO ELSE WOULD SUFFER IF THINGS STAYED THE SAME?

I was becoming the biggest block AND the biggest victim for staying inside my comfort zone. Like there was so much unrealised potential I kept locked inside for NO REASON at all. Laziness and lack of purpose kept me stuck.

My husband would also experience my half-hearted efforts to help him in our coaching business. I would feel competitive against him! And when I would see things weren't done according to my standards, I would end up criticising him instead of helping.

He would also witness my bouts of anger and frustration towards my family member. He would try to act as a go-between, but that only got the ire of this person towards him.

IF YOU DIDN'T CHANGE, WHAT DID YOUR FUTURE LOOK LIKE?

Firstly, I would've seen myself to be an utter failure as a mediocre, ineffective life coach who could not deliver lasting transformations. Despite it being my true passion that brings me fulfilment, I couldn't see myself doing it while feeling so wrecked and angry inside. I couldn't see myself as being a credible and effective coach, because I felt so much incongruence and misalignment within myself.

CRUNCH MOMENT – WHAT WAS THE DEFINING MOMENT THAT MADE YOU DECIDE TO HAVE CREATRIX®?

After my father's funeral in May 2017, I was determined to get up IMMEDIATELY and make things work for my life. I didn't want to stay stuck in resentment, anger and sadness. I didn't want to stay as an angry victim of blame against a family member. I knew that the June 2017 class of Maz was coming up (I had originally wanted to be part of the Feb 2017 batch but my aunt passed away then). I felt that if I delayed any further, it would mean more delays in progressing with my life. There was already too much procrastinating and excuses that got in the way of me, and I've had enough hemming and hawing.

WHAT IS DIFFERENT NOW?

I now have a clear picture and determination to tell the world who I am and what I can do to serve women. Even when it comes to talking about what I do, I no longer have the whiny inner voice that used to say, "Yeah right, you aren't THAT good!" I've been invited to give talks in events and conferences for women.

The confidence and security I feel now is unstoppable!

I feel so much more comfortable in my own skin, and I know I have my place and identity that can stand apart from my husband in terms of the transformation business. My confidence has really been shining through, based on various feedback I'd get from different clients, friends and peers from the coaching and transformation industry. I now also have a weekly 1.5-hour online show on Facebook, where I'm able to reach thousands of people each time.

HOW HAS IT IMPACTED YOUR LOVED ONES?

I'm no longer insecure and resentful when my husband gets invited to speaking gigs and conferences. In fact, I am more supportive of what he's doing (versus before I was feeling competitive).

When it comes to my family member, I am so much calmer with them, and able to crack jokes and tease them in friendly banter. I no longer harbour angry thoughts nor have any resentment towards them at all. I can say that I've totally forgiven them in relation to my dad.

WHAT IS YOUR BIGGEST MESSAGE TO WOMEN WHO HAVE NOT EXPERIENCED A CREATRIX® TRANSFORMATION?

There are so many modalities and therapies out there, but after experiencing Creatrix®, I am totally CONVINCED that there is NOTHING LIKE IT at all in terms of approach, and in terms of results, both immediate and long-term. When it comes to getting unblocked, and resolving deep-seated, deeply rooted emotional issues, I clearly put my confidence and full trust behind Creatrix®. I've seen it work in my life, and I've seen it happen to my clients. I am truly grateful for discovering Maz and her gift. And I am so excited for Creatrix® to be recognised as the biggest and most effective blockbuster therapy for women around the world.

Just GO FOR IT! <3

SAMMY LYNCH, 42

I live with my partner and our two young children and have three older children from a previous marriage.

WHAT WERE THE THREE BIGGEST BLOCKS YOU USED CREATRIX® FOR?

I was afraid of using my voice, not feeling good enough and not believing in myself.

HOW LONG AGO DID YOU HAVE CREATRIX® ON THESE ISSUES?

February 2019.

WHAT ELSE HAD YOU TRIED PRIOR TO CREATRIX®?

Psychologists.

PERSONALLY, WHY DID YOU DECIDE YOU COULDN'T CONTINUE AS YOU WERE?

After seeing psychologists and being on antidepressants in previous years, I didn't wish to go down that route again. I felt like I was just continuously wasting my money and never progressing forward. Due to my passion in natural remedies, I was looking for a natural approach. Forty-one years was long enough to hold on to false beliefs and issues from my past and it was NOW time to let it all go to move forward on a path of peace and joy and to finally enjoy life. With a young son to take care of, I wanted to be the best mum I could be to him and to my older three children and didn't want to drag past relationship issues over into my new relationship. I wanted to get out of bed each morning with a spring in my step and eagerness for the new day ahead instead of dread as I had done for so long in the past.

WHO ELSE WOULD SUFFER IF THINGS STAYED THE SAME?

My kids had a mum full of anxiety who never felt good enough or believed in herself and due to my suffering, they suffered also, as I would be so in my own head that I wasn't present enough for them. I would not follow through with some things due to being so full of anxiety and I didn't want my kids to suffer in the same way and my bad traits to be passed down to them. They deserve a happy mum, a mum who believes in herself to get out of her own way to pave the way and be the role model needed for them to grow into healthy adults.

IF YOU DIDN'T CHANGE, WHAT DID YOUR FUTURE LOOK LIKE?

I would have kept my walls up and eventually I would have made my circle so small I wouldn't have come back from the black hole that swallowed me so many times. I would have slept my life away trying to escape my thoughts and destroyed my family and relationships and not achieved the dreams I had envisioned. I would have been a bad example to my children for them to think this was normal when it was far from it.

CRUNCH MOMENT – WHAT WAS THE DEFINING MOMENT THAT MADE YOU DECIDE TO HAVE CREATRIX®?

I had just come out of a three-year-long court case with a previous partner and I was so over myself that in that moment I knew change had to be made to stop carrying all the issues that seemed to follow me throughout each phase of my life. I had made a few small shifts before clicking that button to commit to an IOWI representative calling me back after going through Maz's short online course. So much of what Maz talked about in how she used to be resonated with me, and I knew this was the last avenue to adventure down to transform me and live my best life, not only for me but for my loved ones.

WHAT IS DIFFERENT NOW?

My voice is heard now. I set boundaries now. After becoming aware that I in fact taught people how to treat me by enabling their behaviour, by never using my voice and just allowing it, I now express myself. I became aware that I am good enough and that issue stemmed from my childhood beliefs of words that I held on to and from having a step-parent where I never felt like part of the family with my half-siblings and not knowing my birth father. I don't have that belief anymore. It was wiped out with my new learnings.

HOW HAS IT IMPACTED YOUR LOVED ONES?

I use my voice and express how I feel now instead of shutting down and shutting off. My relationships are happier and closer, and I am aware that not everything is my fault all the time, and my children won't take on the same trait now. Thank goodness, as my biggest fear was having my children grow up with the same type of issues.

WHAT IS YOUR BIGGEST MESSAGE TO WOMEN WHO HAVE NOT EXPERIENCED A CREATRIX® TRANSFORMATION?

Make this the last ever method you look to in order to break the cycles of beliefs, issues and any inherited traits to live a joyous life for your children and grandchildren. They deserve to live a life of peace, love and happiness just as we do and not take on our issues. If we can break the cycle first, it will have a ripple effect for future generations. Nothing changes if nothing changes. Set your heart free.

SUSAN FARRELL, 55

I live with my beautiful, talented daughter.

WHAT WERE THE THREE BIGGEST BLOCKS YOU USED CREATRIX® FOR?

Rejection, hurt, sad, lonely and it's unfair.

HOW LONG AGO DID YOU HAVE CREATRIX® ON THESE ISSUES?

October 2019.

WHAT ELSE HAD YOU TRIED PRIOR TO CREATRIX®?

Counselling, life coaching, NLP, Time Line Therapy.

WHAT QUALIFICATIONS DID YOU HAVE WHEN YOU TRIED CREATRIX®?

Bachelor of Arts, Diploma of Counselling, Diploma of Life Coaching, Certificate of NLP and Time Line Therapy.

PERSONALLY, WHY DID YOU DECIDE YOU COULDN'T CONTINUE AS YOU WERE?

Something was missing. Stress and trauma would hit me from left field and old behaviours would show up. After

20 years, I just wanted them gone. After a breakup 4.5 years ago, I read about Creatrix® and wanted to try it, as it had the science of epigenetics and biology behind it. It was also created for women, talking to her conscious and unconscious mind simultaneously, using her own intuition and inner wisdom to create profound, lasting change. It was lasting change that I was craving.

WHO ELSE WOULD SUFFER IF THINGS STAYED THE SAME?

My daughter. As a co-parent, I tried to do that role well. I would attempt to keep my feelings of resentment, hurt and rejection out of our conversations. I didn't stop her from seeing her dad. I knew my body language must not be sincere. While I was smiling and appearing to listen, my heart would hurt, and my throat would constrict and the pressure across my chest would feel heavy. I would internalise my pain into mindless chatter of "it wasn't fair". My teeth would grind and tighten, and I would feel the anger rising. It was so hard to move on and I wanted to move on. I was also taking out my pain from a previous partner on my daughter and I had so much regret and remorse from that.

IF YOU DIDN'T CHANGE, WHAT DID YOUR FUTURE LOOK LIKE?

It would continue to be racked with guilt, pain and loneliness. It would weaken the bond I had with my daughter and make co-parenting a living hell.

CRUNCH MOMENT – WHAT WAS THE DEFINING MOMENT THAT MADE YOU DECIDE TO HAVE CREATRIX®?

I was sick and tired of being sick and tired.

WHAT IS DIFFERENT NOW?

I have so much more joy and a better bond with my girl. I listen and enjoy her sharing her time with her father. I get joy from her sharing a story with me, rather than rejection, hurt and resentment.

I am also planning my next chapter and living rather than marking time.

HOW HAS IT IMPACTED YOUR LOVED ONES?

I hope my girl is happier, with a happier mum.

I know I used to take my pain out on her, with reduced patience when I was hurt and sad. To not have that weigh me down anymore, means she gets a healthier, happier more patient mum, who is consciously there for her, rather than being a prisoner to my pain.

WHAT IS YOUR BIGGEST MESSAGE TO WOMEN WHO HAVE NOT EXPERIENCED A CREATRIX® TRANSFORMATION?

I wish Creatrix® had been around 20 years ago and that I had found it. I would have trained in Creatrix® and only Creatrix®. It would have fast-tracked my personal growth and my professional skill set. It would have benefited my clients and me so much earlier.

However, I am glad it finally turned up in my life. Creatrix® has done more for me, in less than 12 months, than counselling, life coaching, NLP and all the self-help books I have bought and the personal development courses I have done in the last 20 years.

Having said that, if I had found Creatrix® 20 years ago, my beautiful daughter may not have existed, so I do not regret a thing, and I am glad Creatrix® is in my life now.

SYLVIA SCHOOFS, 50

Married with two kids and four grandchildren.

WHAT WERE THE THREE BIGGEST BLOCKS YOU USED CREATRIX® FOR?

Not being heard or seen.
Afraid not to be liked.
I'm not good enough.

HOW LONG AGO DID YOU HAVE CREATRIX® ON THESE ISSUES?

March 2017.

WHAT ELSE HAD YOU TRIED PRIOR TO CREATRIX®?

I read a lot of books. I also stepped into several business coaching programs to learn how to run my business properly.

PROFESSIONALLY, WHAT PROMPTED YOU TO SEEK OUT AN ALTERNATIVE TO THE METHODS YOU WERE USING?

My limited beliefs and the way I thought about myself was the reason that kept me away from success, results, moving forward in business.

In my work as a weight consultant, I also searched for a solution that could help my clients. They wanted to lose weight for the wrong reasons. They had beliefs that they only could feel loved by others if they were not overweight, they could only experience happiness in life if they were slim. They had low self-esteem and felt unworthy, hated their bodies, hated themselves because they thought they were failures, and felt totally stressed and frustrated. How on earth can you lose weight if you feel that way? And when you give yourself such a hard time. I was convinced that limited beliefs and negative emotions can settle in your body if you ignore them.

PERSONALLY, WHY DID YOU DECIDE YOU COULDN'T CONTINUE AS YOU WERE?

I was a drama queen. I run up to a wall of my own beliefs and struggles I created myself. I knew that there was an urge to do something about it, otherwise it would end my marriage and I would have to give up my business as well and go back to work. That was not an option to me. Also, I acknowledged that I hold back my emotions and therefore I did not create a bond with my first grandchild. So therefore I put myself on the outs in the family. I created emotional boundaries and therefore I felt very lonesome which, of course, I created myself by not allowing myself to show emotions and feeling not able to receive love.

WHO ELSE WOULD SUFFER IF THINGS STAYED THE SAME?

My husband. We argued all the time and I was emotionally dependent. I needed approval for everything. And therefore I pushed him away instead.

My family because I hold back on them all the time, emotionally. At the time I had only one grandchild but because of my blocks, I was not able to bond.

My dog as well, because he is very sensitive. He was not in a calm state of mind, and very nervous, because I was not in a calm state of mind. My own behaviour reflected to the dog. He was my mirror.

IF YOU DIDN'T CHANGE, WHAT DID YOUR FUTURE LOOK LIKE?

A broken marriage, I think. I had to give up my business and go back to work. I would have ended up as a total emotional wreck, feeling not happy, crying all the time, feeling a complete failure. I really think I may have even ended up in an institution to help me emotionally.

CRUNCH MOMENT – WHAT WAS THE DEFINING MOMENT THAT MADE YOU DECIDE TO HAVE CREATRIX®?

I could not see the strong woman I once was. The optimistic woman. I lost my identity. I hated myself that I couldn't control my emotions. I hated that I could not even clearly see what was mine or from someone else. I was frustrated and stressed. I felt grief that my husband lost the woman he once married. I knew something HAD to happen or I would have lost everything.

WHAT IS DIFFERENT NOW?

From an insecure and emotional woman, I've been transformed into a confident, powerful woman. I no longer make choices based on negative thoughts. I do not need approval or permission from someone else. I make decisions of my own. I feel released, free. No more inner voices, and I'm rarely stressed. I finally have and feel the connection with myself, my inner wisdom, and therefore I am connected with my beloveds! My first grandchild still is a little cautious, but our bond has changed. After my Creatrix® experience, three other grandchildren came along, and they adore me. It is really different compared to my first grandchild. My dog is calm. There is peace in my relationship now. Everything is the complete opposite of how it was. I'm feeling very grateful that I had a breakthrough.

HOW HAS IT IMPACTED YOUR LOVED ONES?

No more emotional discussions with my husband. And if he is struggling and has a bad day and he tries to trigger me, I am able to receive his words in a different way. I also clearly see what he is doing and what's his, so therefore I do not feel responsible for his feelings or for him feeling bad. It is his struggle, not mine. It does not influence me in any way. Of course I support him, but I won't receive it in that way.

I'm feeling really confident that whatever I do or whatever I decide is just fine. Trusting my gut is a gift. I'm thankful that I'm able to listen to my gut. It is a release to let out emotions and not even feel it anymore.

I have a different bond with my whole family, and they see and acknowledge the change. It gives us peace. There is more living in the now, in the moment, not constantly worrying about the future or what to do. The change is really amazing. It's the total opposite of what it was. Knowing what the differences are between male and female helps to understand the difference in communication and focus, for instance. Knowing how the cycle impacts your life and emotions helps to go with the flow and not fight it.

WHAT IS YOUR BIGGEST MESSAGE TO WOMEN WHO HAVE NOT EXPERIENCED A CREATRIX® TRANSFORMATION?

Please do yourself a favour and at least examine what this can do for you. There is no need to be stuck. There IS a way out! And when Creatrix® crosses your path, you have found the real solution!

Do not compare it to other methods that look similar. Because they're not!

It has not only profits for you but for all people around you love. And can you already see the pattern that runs in the family from your behaviour? What would it mean to you if you can break through the pattern? Your children do not have to live the same pattern as soon as you clean up the past.

TAMMY KERR, 43

Married to a firefighter and farmer and we have two teenage boys.

WHAT WERE THE THREE BIGGEST BLOCKS YOU USED CREATRIX® FOR?

I was stuck. I knew what I needed to do to become healthier, but I kept self-sabotaging myself.

I felt like a hypocrite. I work in the health and healing industry, but I was not doing what I was asking my clients to do.

I had a huge unknown unconscious fear of change. I feared the unknown and this stopped me from stepping out and doing everything I desperately wanted to do for myself, my family, my new business and my life purpose.

HOW LONG AGO DID YOU HAVE CREATRIX® ON THESE ISSUES?

February 2020.

WHAT ELSE HAD YOU TRIED PRIOR TO CREATRIX®?

Journalling for over 10 years, counselling for five years, self-help/personal growth books.

WHAT QUALIFICATIONS DID YOU HAVE WHEN YOU TRIED CREATRIX®?

Reiki master, remedial massage therapist, Angel Intuitive and Healer.

PROFESSIONALLY, WHAT PROMPTED YOU TO SEEK OUT AN ALTERNATIVE TO THE METHODS YOU WERE USING?

I could see in other people that issues lay deep in the subconscious realm that affected every aspect of their life, health and happiness, and I knew there was a tool that could address these issues and assist deep healing. I knew Creatrix® was this missing link when I saw it and my gut told me it was the answer to my issues and those of my clients, so I took a leap of faith and am so incredibly grateful that I did because I am now able to facilitate that deep healing with my sisters who are also ready to step up and awaken to their greatness.

PERSONALLY, WHY DID YOU DECIDE YOU COULDN'T CONTINUE AS YOU WERE?

My level of personal frustration was at an all-time high. I was really angry at myself, floundering in the same spot day after day when I wanted to break free from the chains that invisibly weighed me down. I knew I couldn't see MY issues. I had tried to DO IT ON MY OWN for a long, long time, and it hadn't worked. I knew I had a purpose to help others but in order to do that, I needed to help myself first.

WHO ELSE WOULD SUFFER IF THINGS STAYED THE SAME?

When someone suffers, everyone around them suffers, even when they try to mask it and cover it with a smiling face or a joke and a laugh. When you suffer, your light is dim, and you cannot shine onto those who need you. Being a mum, everyone relies on you being at your best all the time. To me, that meant I needed to be the real me, however, that was in each and every given moment. Not faking it when I was sad or pretending I was okay when I was not. Being comfortable in my skin and with my feelings was a necessity to me so they would know it was okay for them to feel all the emotions we were born to feel. Having a family of males around me, I knew I wanted them to grow up into confident, emotionally intelligent males who felt comfortable expressing their deepest emotions, and I needed to be able to role model that for them. Now I am less reactionary and own my truth allowing my boys to do the same.

IF YOU DIDN'T CHANGE, WHAT DID YOUR FUTURE LOOK LIKE?

I would have most likely divorced. We had been on the edge of separating for a few years, because of the way I perceived my husband and marriage. I felt really powerless and had more than a few beliefs that were not healthy to a long-lasting happy marriage. I actually thought having Creatrix® might be the thing that empowered me to leave but actually it empowered me to see things with such clarity that I had never experienced before.

CRUNCH MOMENT – WHAT WAS THE DEFINING MOMENT THAT MADE YOU DECIDE TO HAVE CREATRIX®?

I was sitting talking with a friend, and we were complaining that we both knew how to lose weight and exercise, but for some unknown reason, we just couldn't, didn't, wouldn't. I was fuming and sick of failing and feeling like there was something seriously wrong with me. Why couldn't I JUST DO IT? (like the bloody NIKE ad says!) I vowed to her that I would find the answer to why we were stuck, and when I did, I would share it with her and all the other stuck women in the world. So when I saw the ad, I knew it was my answer.

WHAT IS DIFFERENT NOW?

Everything. I have so much forward momentum and energy. My life is how I wished it could be and now I am living that life. I had anxiety from the moment I woke till I went to sleep. I even dreamt of food sometimes. I honestly hated food and now I love and enjoy it. I also love and enjoy life more than I did before. Everything feels brighter, lighter and freer. The littlest things make me smile and I sing all the time now, just because. I am just so much happier and feel genuinely fulfilled in my life.

HOW HAS IT IMPACTED YOUR LOVED ONES?

They are all happier because I am happier. I am more stable, so I bring balance and harmony to our family now, and I am definitely more fun to be around. I don't stress about all the little things I once did, and I am not on my husband's back like I once was. I am a fun mum, wife, sister, friend and daughter, who is able to express myself with kindness and compassion on a new level.

WHAT IS YOUR BIGGEST MESSAGE TO WOMEN WHO HAVE NOT EXPERIENCED A CREATRIX® TRANSFORMATION?

The unknown is scary. You are stronger and braver than you think. Take your sister's hand and trust that she will not let you fall. She has your back and will fight beside you to bring you through the darkness and into the light. It is our greatest privilege and honour to walk with you as you undertake this almighty journey. We know you will love yourself and your life on the other side of this transformation. As women it is our time to heal the generational wounds and patterns so we can set ourselves and those who come after us free.

You are worth it. You always have been worth it. You have gifts the world needs right now. Let's be brave and break free together FOREVER.

TRACY HANDLEY, 43

Married with three boys.

___

WHAT WERE THE THREE BIGGEST BLOCKS YOU USED CREATRIX® FOR?

I felt guilty for my brother's death, blaming myself.
Resentment from being in an abusive relationship, the hurt and shame I went through.
Not good enough; I never felt good enough in any part of my life, no matter what it was.

HOW LONG AGO DID YOU HAVE CREATRIX® ON THESE ISSUES?

December 2019.

WHAT ELSE HAD YOU TRIED PRIOR TO CREATRIX®?

Counselling and hypnotherapy.

PERSONALLY, WHY DID YOU DECIDE YOU COULDN'T CONTINUE AS YOU WERE?

I had hit rock bottom. I was withdrawn from everyone or a raging lunatic. There was no in-between. I was an emotional wreck, I would cry all the time, or I would be screaming at everyone in my path. It hit me when my husband said to me, "You need help, I can't do this any longer. If you don't get help, then I am done and this marriage is over." This really hurt because I knew he was serious and I didn't want to lose him or feel like this, I just didn't know how to fix it.

WHO ELSE WOULD SUFFER IF THINGS STAYED THE SAME?

Everyone around me. I was not a nice person to be around. My emotions ran wild and I was out of control. My family, my kids, work colleagues, but most of all my husband was suffering and didn't know what to do, so he shut himself off.

IF YOU DIDN'T CHANGE, WHAT DID YOUR FUTURE LOOK LIKE?

What future? I really don't think it would have been much of a life. If I didn't change, I would have lost everyone who was important to me. Why would anyone stay in my life if I hated it myself? I didn't want to be here at all.

CRUNCH MOMENT – WHAT WAS THE DEFINING MOMENT THAT MADE YOU DECIDE TO HAVE CREATRIX®?

My crunch moment was when I had really lost my sh**, I was raging mad, yelling and screaming like a full-on nut job and not thinking at all about what I was saying. It was really hurtful, nasty stuff, and the next day I felt sick. I thought, "What the hell is wrong with ME? I need help." My husband was ready to leave me and I still had no control. I wanted nothing more than to get rid of all the guilt, resentment and not feeling good enough to disappear so I could be happy, live the life I deserved and love the people in my life fully.

WHAT IS DIFFERENT NOW?

NOW, life is fantastic. I am in a great place. I have learnt how to handle my emotions and to think about how I am going to react. I have a great relationship with everyone around me now. I am so much more understanding, calmer and have more respect towards everyone. Because I am much nicer to be around, the ripple effect has really been noticeable, and everyone else is much happier too. I love the woman I am today.

HOW HAS IT IMPACTED YOUR LOVED ONES?

My loved ones were really worried about me and my mental health. It was really hard on them to see me spiralling out of control and they had no idea how to help. Now that they have the relaxed, happy and chill woman back, they are relieved, more relaxed and happy. No more walking around on eggshells waiting for the next outburst.

WHAT IS YOUR BIGGEST MESSAGE TO WOMEN WHO HAVE NOT EXPERIENCED A CREATRIX® TRANSFORMATION?

It is the best experience that has ever happened to me. I would not like to think of where I would be now without it. Creatrix® made me feel whole and complete; it was life-changing. It saved my marriage, and it saved me.

It truly is the most amazing tool in the world with REAL, LONG-LASTING RESULTS.

Every women needs to experience Creatrix®. It is fast, safe and designed for women by a woman. You won't ever need anything else.

YOLANDE GARRICK, 48

I live with my partner and I have two adult kids and two grandsons.

WHAT WERE THE THREE BIGGEST BLOCKS YOU USED CREATRIX® FOR?

At the time, I wanted to start my own business, but I was consumed with the fear of failure, self-doubt and the fear of success. This kept me stuck and forever questioning myself.

HOW LONG AGO DID YOU HAVE CREATRIX® ON THESE ISSUES?

May 2018.

WHAT ELSE HAD YOU TRIED PRIOR TO CREATRIX®?

As an avid learner, I threw myself into personal development for years. I did The Forum, Advanced Leadership and Communication Course with Landmark education. I also tried life coaching, Time Line Therapy and hypnosis.

WHAT QUALIFICATIONS DID YOU HAVE WHEN YOU TRIED CREATRIX®?

Personal trainer and weight loss consultant, wellness coach, Passion Test Facilitator.

PROFESSIONALLY, WHAT PROMPTED YOU TO SEEK OUT AN ALTERNATIVE TO THE METHODS YOU WERE USING?

Everything I had tried worked to a certain extent, BUT the fear and negative emotions were much deeper than the conscious level I had been working at to try and overcome these. I needed something that worked at a much deeper level.

PERSONALLY, WHY DID YOU DECIDE YOU COULDN'T CONTINUE AS YOU WERE?

I knew that if I didn't do everything in my power to overcome these limiting beliefs, that I would end up resentful and disappointed. I had to do it for my kids too. I had to be the change in our family and be that person that breaks the cycle of doubt and fear.

WHO ELSE WOULD SUFFER IF THINGS STAYED THE SAME?

I knew that my kids would always know that I held back from pursuing my passion because of doubt and fear, and I did not want this to be the reason they didn't live a purposeful life.

IF YOU DIDN'T CHANGE, WHAT DID YOUR FUTURE LOOK LIKE?

I would always feel like a part of me was never complete, like something would be missing. It was that part of me that knew she was capable of great things but never got to experience it. I would have resigned myself to an average life but be unfulfilled. Resentment, disappointment, and failure would have taken over me eventually.

CRUNCH MOMENT – WHAT WAS THE DEFINING MOMENT THAT MADE YOU DECIDE TO HAVE CREATRIX®?

Once I had spoken to one of the program advisors, I knew that this was something I had to do. Call it gut instinct or an inner knowing, but I knew it was something I could trust. Being a very logical thinker and after watching the videos and understanding the difference between what was being offered against what I had already done, it just made sense to me. I knew that this was a defining moment that was going to change my life.

WHAT IS DIFFERENT NOW?

I finally feel like I have connected with my true self. At 47 years of age, I feel like my life is just starting. I have realised that all that I ever needed was always within me, and Creatrix® helped me find it. I'm aligned with my passion of empowering women and I do it with ease.

HOW HAS IT IMPACTED YOUR LOVED ONES?

My relationship with my partner is amazing. I have a relationship I never thought was possible and I realise that the whole time it was me getting in the way of that before. It's happy, playful, loving, healthy and strong. My kids see me following my passion and are so proud of me. I know that they will always remember me as someone who never gave up and followed her passion, which is all I want for them too.

WHAT IS YOUR BIGGEST MESSAGE TO WOMEN WHO HAVE NOT EXPERIENCED A CREATRIX® TRANSFORMATION?

Trust your gut and let that make your decision for you. You know that deep down inside that this makes sense. You know that something like this has been long overdue and like everything that has real purpose and meaning, it is always going to ask something extra of you. This is that defining moment. Just back yourself and take that leap of faith. I PROMISE you will not be disappointed. Do it for YOU.

DEMI WONE, 31

Independent fur Mumma of 3.

3 ISSUES – WHAT WERE THE 3 BIGGEST BLOCKS YOU USED CREATRIX FOR?

Resentment at the life I'd been given, abandonment and disappointment.

HOW LONG AGO DID YOU HAVE CREATRIX ON THESE ISSUES?

May 2018.

WHAT ELSE HAD YOU TRIED PRIOR TO HAVING CREATRIX?

NLP, Hypnotherapy, Counselling, Psychology, Antidepressants.

WHAT QUALIFICATIONS DID YOU HAVE WHEN YOU TRIED CREATRIX?

NLP Practitioner, Hypnotherapist.

PROFESSIONALLY, WHAT PROMPTED YOU TO SEEK OUT AN ALTERNATIVE TO THE METHODS YOU WERE USING? (IF APPLICABLE)

I had studied previously in the above methods but never followed through with a business helping others because the courses just didn't offer enough competency or support for me to feel like I could go out and help others. The Creatrix® Transformology® Program was so different, I felt confident and competent.

HOW LONG AGO DID YOU HAVE CREATRIX ON THESE ISSUES?

May 2018.

PERSONALLY, WHY DID YOU DECIDE YOU COULDN'T CONTINUE AS YOU WERE?

I had tried all the things, nothing ever worked long term. I had a traumatic, crazy childhood and I reached the age of 18, looked at all the "normal" people around me and I just couldn't work out how to be like them. I was so broken, so I went searching. Doctors didn't seem to know how to help me, except to offer pills. I remember one psychologist basically told me he was in over his head with me and I needed someone who could handle my trauma. That experience sent me into a tailspin for years. NLP and hypno didn't stick, they were eye opening and my entry into finally helping myself, but it was demoralising when the patterns started to reassert themselves a few months later. It took me a long time to try something else, Creatrix® was that thing and it changed everything.

WHO ELSE WAS SUFFERING IF YOU STAYED THE SAME?

Every single person who came into contact with me. I was seriously hard to love. I was so defensive, snippy, snarky, judgemental, negative – I brought that to everyone in my life.

IF YOU DIDN'T CHANGE WHAT DID YOUR FUTURE LOOK LIKE?

I would have been utterly miserable, never left my tiny little world that was becoming tinier and tinier the more I pushed people away and let my anxieties grow. My panic attacks were worsening, I could barely even go do grocery shopping, I would panic just finding a carpark.

CRUNCH MOMENT – What was the defining moment that made you decide to do it in that moment?

I knew I was always meant for more than the little life I was leading, I was so unhappy, becoming more and more negative, I sucked the fun out of the room. In the end, my partner at the time told me he was sick of how horribly unhappy I was, so I quit my job, took some time and started to find me, my empathy and my value.

WHAT IS DIFFERENT NOW?

Everything.

Sexual abuse, physical abuse, bullying, being abandoned as a child over and over, domestic violence, going on the run, moving around all the time, never feeling stable – all of those things now live exactly where they should, in the past. Not one little bit of charge lives in my body when I think of any of it. I'm truly free. I never thought this was truly, truly possible.

I now live on my own, no one else pays my bills and I have built a comfortable, stable, independent, adventurous, joy filled, peaceful, fulfilling life. I will never need a "safe" 9-5 soul sucking job again because I absolutely know I can do what I've chosen to do, helping other women. It brings me so much fulfillment. I never had the confidence to do that before.

I love EVERY SINGLE DAY of my existence. I used to live with this constant anxiety, it was like a burning in the top of my stomach and I'd get adrenaline shocks throughout my body constantly from panic. All day, every day. I always felt on edge, defensive and if anything went wrong, I would just explode or implode. I feel so at peace in my own body now, there is no charge. None. I haven't had a panic attack in three years. That's not to say I've become some lah-lah airy fairy robot, it's so much better than that – I feel so much MORE, but it's a good feeling. I feel content and peaceful AND motivated at the same time - a natural balance of being present and pushing myself towards what I want.

Since my breakthrough, I've been through explosive break ups, multiple back-to-back operations, loss and many other trials and I just handled it. I didn't bury it or go into old patterns, I just got it done and moved on. My resilience is out of this world, Creatrix® didn't falter once.

HOW HAS IT IMPACTED YOUR LOVED ONES?

I never really felt like I "fit" anywhere. I'm a little bit of everything, a bit of a maverick or a chameleon, probably because we moved around so much growing up. Because of that, I never really found out who I was, what I wanted, what I liked. Now that I truly know me, I have found the most beautiful, supportive, true people to surround myself with. The Demi they get is a Demi you would WANT to be around. I used to speak fear into people's plans and ideas, I'm now everyone's biggest cheerleader. I like who I am now.

WHAT IS YOUR BIGGEST MESSAGE TO WOMEN WHO HAVE NOT EXPERIENCED A CREATRIX TRANSFORMATION?

There will always be ten million reasons to not fully commit to healing yourself right now, next week, next year. YOU are the only one who can call it and decide enough is enough. I promise, it will change EVERYTHING and it'll be beyond anything you could have imagined.

CONTACT US

To experience a breakthrough like these women have, go to the Creatrix® Transformologist® who may have referred this book to you.

If you don't know a Transformologist® go to:

        www.instituteofwomen.com

If you're interested in learning more about the Institute of Women International™ and how you can become a Creatrix® Transformologist® and help other women to get results like these, please go to:

        www.instituteofwomen.com

To learn more about Maz Schirmer visit:

        www.mazschirmer.com.au

www.ingramcontent.com/pod-product-compliance
Lightning Source LLC
Chambersburg PA
CBHW050312010526
44107CB00055B/2212